Marie-Pierre BESSON DE VEZAC

War and Artificial Intelligence

Marie-Pierre BESSON DE VEZAC

War and Artificial Intelligence

Autonomous weapons systems and other issues

ScienciaScripts

Imprint

Cover image: www.ingimage.com

This book is a translation from the original published under ISBN 978-3-8381-4392-7.

Publisher:
Sciencia Scripts
is a trademark of
Dodo Books Indian Ocean Ltd. and OmniScriptum S.R.L publishing group

120 High Road, East Finchley, London, N2 9ED, United Kingdom
Str. Armeneasca 28/1, office 1, Chisinau MD-2012, Republic of Moldova, Europe
Managing Directors: Ieva Konstantinova, Victoria Ursu
info@omniscriptum.com

Printed at: see last page
ISBN: 978-620-6-76364-2

Contents

"Artificial intelligence could well make war more deadly, but also more precise. The idea of machines that can make decisions about life and death raises profound ethical questions. If these decisions escape human control, war could become an automated process, where the absurdity of human violence is amplified by the cold logic of algorithms."

Harari Yuval Noah,

Homo Deus: A brief history of the future

Introduction

Artificial intelligence (AI) refers to computer systems capable of performing tasks usually carried out by humans, such as recognising speech, decisions or analysing complex data. AI is based on algorithms and automatic learning models, which enable machines to "understand", learn and adapt to new information without direct human intervention. It is used in a variety of fields, from medicine to finance, and is beginning to play an increasingly important role in warfare.

Artificial intelligence in warfare refers to the use of autonomous or semi-autonomous technologies to carry out military missions. This includes weapons systems, drones, robots and command software that can analyse data, predict threats and make decisions autonomously or with assistance. AI can make military operations more effective, but raises ethical questions about accountability, safety, and human control over life-or-death decisions in conflict contexts.

The evolution of armed conflicts has been marked by a constant transformation of strategies, technologies and political, economic and social issues. From ancient confrontations to contemporary hybrid wars, military conflicts have followed a trajectory shaped by technical innovations, geopolitical changes and evolutions in military doctrines.

Today, modern conflicts are characterised by a combination of military, technological and informational threats. Hybrid wars, as illustrated by the tensions in Ukraine and the Middle East, show that confrontations are no longer limited to traditional battlefields, but also economic warfare, cyber attacks and disinformation campaigns. The emergence of new military powers and growing geopolitical rivalries underline the fact that the conflicts of the 21st century will be marked by an ever greater integration of technology, political strategy and psychological warfare.

The evolution of armed conflict reflects the changes in human society, with every technological advance and geopolitical shift influencing the way wars are fought. From war of movement to information warfare, confrontations are becoming ever more complex, requiring constant adaptation of military doctrines and defence strategies.

But the greatest challenge remains that of artificial intelligence, which is increasingly used in armed conflicts.

The development of artificial intelligence (AI) technologies is profoundly transforming military strategies and the conduct of armed conflicts. Once relegated to the realms of science fiction, AI is now a reality that influences military decision-making, the analysis of strategic data and even the execution of combat operations. From autonomous drones to algorithm-assisted command systems, AI is gradually permeating every aspect of modern conflict.

The development of artificial intelligence in the military sphere raises complex issues that go beyond the simple technological framework to touch on profound ethical, political and strategic issues. While advances in AI promise to improve the accuracy of strikes and optimise on the battlefield, they are also accompanied by fears linked to the growing autonomy of weapons systems and their implications for the conduct of modern warfare.

One of the arguments in favour of integrating AI into military systems is the reduction in human casualties. By improving real-time data analysis, optimising target recognition and reducing the time taken to react to threats, these technologies can help avoid costly human errors and increase effectiveness of operations. Autonomous drones, for example, offer the possibility of carrying out dangerous missions without directly exposing soldiers, thereby reducing the risk to the armed forces. Artificial intelligence also makes it possible to analyse massive quantities of information from sensors, satellites and open sources to better anticipate enemy movements and adopt appropriate strategies. The idea that decisions based on accurate analytical models can limit collateral damage and avoid civilian casualties is an argument frequently put forward by supporters of military AI.

However, this optimistic vision comes up against major concerns about the dehumanisation of conflicts. Entrusting life and death to machines raises a fundamental moral issue: an AI, however advanced, has no conscience or sense of discernment. It cannot interpret the context with the same sensitivity as a human being and does not understand the ethical nuances that may surround an act of war. Excessive automation of military decisions can lead to situations where innocent civilians are targeted because of algorithmic errors or misinterpretations of system data. The ability of an algorithm to distinguish a combatant from a non-combatant is based solely on programmed criteria, which may be biased or unsuited to complex situations.

Algorithmic biases are another source of concern. Military AI is trained on data sets that often reflect human assumptions and biases. If these biases are not identified and corrected, they can result in erroneous decisions in the field. A facial recognition system used to identify enemy targets may, for example, be influenced by biased data that results in incorrect identification, leading to unjustified strikes. These biases are not always immediately detectable and can cause disasters before their effects are even understood. In addition, the speed with which ΓIA can make decisions prevent human intervention in the event of error, increasing the potential for uncontrollable blunders.

The risk of hacking is another major problem. The more a military system relies on artificial intelligence, the more vulnerable it becomes to cyber attacks. An adversary could try to disrupt or manipulate the algorithms used by an army to make it take the wrong decisions or to use autonomous weapons against its own forces. In a context of electronic warfare and hybrid confrontations, the security of AI systems becomes a critical issue, as a simple hack can trigger uncontrolled reprisals or cause massive loss of life. The growing interconnection between defence systems, satellites and autonomous weapons is creating an environment where a well-coordinated computer attack can paralyse an adversary without even a physical battle taking place.

Politically, the integration of AI into the military raises questions of responsibility and control. Who should be held responsible when an autonomous weapon makes a mistake? The manufacturer of the software, the army that uses it, or the programmer who designed the algorithm?

The lack of a clear legal framework for these new technologies further complicates the situation. Many experts are calling for international regulations to limit the use of autonomous weapons and guarantee systematic human control over critical decisions. However, the arms race in the field of military FIA complicates the implementation of such regulations. The major powers are investing massively in these technologies, each fearing that they will fall behind their adversaries, which is leading to accelerated development without any real consideration of the long-term risks.

The geopolitical implications of the development of military AI should not be underestimated. The emergence of these technologies may alter the balance of power between nations and lead to a new form of deterrence based on technological superiority. States equipped with the most advanced AI systems may be tempted to conduct more aggressive military operations, knowing that their losses would be limited. Conversely, non-state actors, such as terrorist groups or criminal organisations, may seek to exploit these technologies to carry out large-scale automated attacks. Increasing access to artificial intelligence algorithms and cheap drone technologies raises the possibility of conflicts where armed groups use swarms of autonomous drones to strike targets in a coordinated manner, making war even more difficult to control.

Faced with these challenges, the question of how to regulate military AI is becoming crucial. Should autonomous weapons be banned outright, as some humanitarian organisations and international institutions are calling for? Or should their use simply be regulated to ensure sufficient human control? The answer to these questions will largely depend on the political and ethical choices made by governments, as well as the pressure exerted by civil society to impose strict rules on the use of these technologies. The balance between military effectiveness and respect for ethical principles is a central dilemma that will influence the wars of tomorrow.

The development of AI in the military field is now accompanied by a multi-faceted debate, where technological promises and ethical risks collide. While these tools can improve the accuracy of operations and limit human losses on the part of the armed forces, they also raise profound questions about the responsibility, security and morality of modern conflicts. The development of these technologies must be carefully managed to avoid war becoming a field of action in which vital decisions are taken by machines with no awareness or real understanding of the human issues at stake.

Moreover, one of the main arguments in favour of strict regulation, or even a ban on autonomous weapons, is the fear of uncontrolled proliferation of these technologies. As AI systems become more accessible and cheaper, non-state groups or malicious actors may acquire technologies that would enable them to carry autonomous attacks. Terrorist organisations, for example, may use drones or combat robots to carry out strikes without human intervention, increasing the risk of asymmetric warfare and conflicts that destabilise regions and civilian populations. The issue of controlling these technologies is therefore becoming a priority for those who fear their use for malicious purposes, but also a source of new inequalities in the distribution of military capabilities, as the richest and most technologically advanced nations continue to dominate the arena.

Despite these concerns, the lack of an international consensus on the regulation of autonomous weapons makes it difficult to develop a comprehensive legal framework for their use. The negotiations in this area are often marked by divergent national interests and contradictory approaches to security. The main obstacle lies in the complex balance between national sovereignty and international responsibility. States are reluctant to accept binding restrictions on the development of technologies that they believe may strengthen their national security. Some countries consider that regulations imposed by international organisations may hamper their ability to defend their strategic interests, or even to counter technologically more advanced adversaries.

For several years, the UN has been aware of the need to define a legal framework for autonomous weapons. In 2018, the Group of Governmental Experts (GGE) on Autonomous Lateral Weapons (LAWS) was formed within the framework of the Convention on Certain Conventional Weapons (CCW). The purpose of this group is to discuss the implications of autonomous weapons and to determine best practices for their regulation. At the 2019 Meeting of the States Parties to the CCW, a number of countries expressed their concern about the uncontrolled development of these weapons and called for strict regulation or even a complete ban. However, these discussions have met with resistance from certain States, particularly those that invest massively in these technologies, such as the United States, China and Russia, which are reluctant to accept overly restrictive restrictions on their military capabilities.

Despite these efforts, the lack of consensus remains a major obstacle. In 2018, at a meeting of the Convention on Certain Conventional Weapons, some States proposed tougher regulation of autonomous weapons, limiting their development to non-lethal missions only or imposing transparency criteria on the algorithms used for decision-making . Other countries, on the other hand, have refused to commit to a total ban or even to strict regulation. The United States, for example, has rejected a ban on látal autonomous weapons, arguing that these technologies could be used to benefit its armed forces and did not require restrictions outside existing humanitarian rules. In addition, some Member States fear that too strict a regulation would prevent them from maintaining their military and technological competitiveness, particularly in the face of adversaries continue to develop autonomous weapons without international control.

The debate within the UN has also raised complex questions about responsibility for violations of international law. If an autonomous weapon makes a mistake, who is responsible? Developed countries are insisting on the importance of maintaining human control over military decisions, stressing that ultimate responsibility must rest with a human operator, even if the technology allows considerable autonomy of action. This principle has been put forward by several experts in international humanitarian law, who point out that the laws of war are based on the fundamental principles of distinction, proportionality and necessity, principles that are difficult to apply to machines that lack moral and contextual judgement.

At the same time, the International Committee of the Red Cross (ICRC) and other humanitarian organisations have stepped up their efforts to raise awareness of the need for strict regulation of autonomous weapons. These organisations stress that autonomous weapons risk undermining the foundations of international humanitarian law, in particular the rule that military force must always be used with discretion and under human control. Their aim is to put pressure on States to accept a comprehensive legal framework that would ensure that autonomous weapons cannot be used to inflict unnecessary or unjustified suffering on civilian populations.

However, despite resolutions and debates on the subject, the process remains extremely slow and difficult, as it is subject to pressure from the major military powers, which often resist the idea of external control over their military capabilities. In the absence of a binding global treaty, the United Nations is struggling to define guidelines accepted by all member states.

The challenge is also a practical one: how can we verify that weapons systems comply international humanitarian standards? The effective implementation of regulation requires complex monitoring and control mechanisms, capable of keeping pace with the involution of technologies while guaranteeing transparency and accountability. But the speed of innovation in the field of AI makes this task particularly difficult. It is also difficult to design a legal framework that is applicable to all types of autonomous weapon systems, whether they be drones, land combat robots or autonomous maritime systems, without running the risk of leaving loopholes in control of constantly evolving technologies.

The issue of regulating autonomous weapons systems continues to divide the international community. Although the debate is moving slowly, decisions in this area will be crucial for the future of warfare, international security and human rights. Striking a balance between the need to guarantee the security of states and the protection of civilians, while ensuring ethical control over the technologies of warfare, represents one of the greatest challenges facing international diplomacy in the 21st century.

This book explains the challenges posed by the integration of AI into the military domain from the perspective international humanitarian law and general international law. It will analyse the fundamental principles of IHL, the impact of autonomous technologies on the conduct of hostilities, and efforts to regulate their development. Using an interdisciplinary approach, we will attempt to answer a key question: how can technological progress be reconciled with respect for the rules established to limit the ravages of war?

CHAPTER 1

Artificial intelligence in armed conflicts

Artificial intelligence is playing an increasingly central role in the military, revolutionising the way conflicts are fought and security is assured. Its integration into the armed forces covers a broad spectrum applications, ranging from automatic target recognition and lethal autonomous weapon systems (SALA) to strategic data analysis, cyber security and military logistics.

One of the first areas where artificial intelligence is being used massively in the military sector is **automatic target recognition,** a technology that is revolutionising the way armed forces collect, process and exploit information in real time. introduction of AI in this field is based primarily on advances in computer vision, deep learning and the fusion of data from multiple sources. These advances are helping to optimise the surveillance and tracking of targets, making military operations more precise and effective.

One of the main advantages artificial intelligence in target recognition lies in its ability to process immense quantities of data in record time. Traditionally, the analysis of satellite or aerial images required the intervention of human analysts, a laborious and time-consuming task that was prone to misinterpretation. Today, thanks machine learning algorithms and deep neural networks, armies can automate this task and obtain results in a matter of seconds, or even in real time. AI can analyse images from spy satellites, reconnaissance drones or even cameras on land and air vehicles, instantly identifying anomalies, suspicious movements or concentrations of enemy troops.

This technology goes far beyond the simple detection objects. Thanks to advanced recognition models, AI is able to accurately identify specific vehicles, strategic infrastructures or even suspicious individuals on the basis of physical or behavioural characteristics. For example, in anti-terrorist operations, AI can analyse video footage recorded by drones and spot unusual behaviour, such as grouped movements in sensitive areas, the use of military equipment or even the modification of traffic patterns. Such systems are already in use in several of the world's armies, including the United States, Israel and China, where they play a key role in surveillance and intervention strategies.

Modern military drones[1] , such as the MQ-9 Reaper used by the US army or the Harop drone developed by Israel Aerospace Industries, incorporate these intelligent reconnaissance systems. These aircraft are capable operating at high altitude and carrying out prolonged surveillance missions without requiring constant human intervention. By combining AI with infrared sensors, synthetic aperture radar and other advanced detection technologies, they can identify targets with remarkable accuracy, even in adverse weather conditions or in the presence of electronic jamming countermeasures.

One of the major advantages of this technology is its ability to distinguish military targets from civilian populations, thereby reducing the risk of collateral casualties and improving the ethics of military operations. Artificial intelligence can compare captured images with databases containing information on civilian infrastructures, hospitals or schools, ensuring that strikes are directed only against legitimate military targets. This feature is particularly crucial in modern conflicts, where fighting often takes place in urban areas and the presence of non-combatants complicates operational decisions.

However, despite these advances, the automatic recognition of targets by AI raises significant challenges and risks. One of the major problems concerns the reliability of algorithms and the management of potential errors. Although AI systems are

---

1 See my book "Drone and the Law of Waar", 2025.

extremely powerful, they are not infallible and can be subject to algorithmic bias, leading to erroneous identifications. Misclassifying a target, for example by mistaking a civilian vehicle for a military one, can have dramatic consequences in the field.

Another major issue is the **risk of hacking and manipulation of AI systems.** In a cyber-war context, adversaries may try exploit the flaws in the algorithms by supplying them with falsified data or by launching attacks against image processing systems. Techniques such as data poisoning, which consists of introducing errors into the training sets of AI models, can alter their performance and compromise their effectiveness.

The legal and ethical dimensions of the use of AI in target recognition are also at the heart of international concerns. At present, the regulatory frameworks governing the use of these technologies in conflict situations remain vague and underdeveloped. While some countries advocate strict regulation to limit the risks of abuse and error, others favour the unrestricted development of these tools in order to retain a strategic advantage . The United Nations, through initiatives such as the Convention on Certain Conventional Weapons, is attempting establish a dialogue on the use of autonomous weapons and IA-assisted reconnaissance technologies, but an international consensus is struggling to emerge.

Finally, the increasing autonomy of AI-based reconnaissance systems raises the question of the role of humans in military decision-making. As these technologies become more sophisticated, there is a risk that military commands will increasingly rely on the recommendations of algorithms without questioning their analyses. This over-reliance on AI could lead to a dilution of responsibility in , particularly in the event of blunders or violations of international humanitarian law.

Artificial intelligence (IA) is increasingly integrated into contemporary military operations, particularly for automatic target recognition. This technology enables armed forces analyse massive volumes of data in real time from a variety of sources, such as satellites, drones and ground sensors, in order accurately identify enemy vehicles, strategic infrastructure or suspicious individuals.

In Ukraine, since 2022[2] , more than 2 million hours drone videos have been collected to train AI models. These systems help to identify targets, assess the effectiveness of weapons and make strategic decisions. For example, organisations such as OCHI centralise and analyse these video streams from more than 15,000 drone crews, improving efficiency on the battlefield.

Israel has also integrated AI[3] into its military operations, particularly during conflicts with Hamas. Systems such as "Habsora" and "Lavender" have been used to generate lists of targets to strike, y including buildings and individuals affiliated to Hamas. This approach enabled targets to be identified more quickly and accurately, increasing the effectiveness of air strikes.

These examples illustrate how AI is being used in current conflicts to improve target recognition, optimise military operations and boost effectiveness on the ground.

The use of artificial intelligence (AI) in the military field is not limited to threat recognition or detection, but also extends to the **planning and command of military operations,** transforming the way armies design and execute their strategies. By exploiting machine learning , armed forces can enemy behaviour, predict their future actions and adapt their own operations in real time. AI then becomes a strategic ally in optimising resources, reducing

---

2 Agence Reuters, 20 December 2024

3 French daily "Le Monde" "On the battlefield, AI is surpassing the military's expectations".

risks and improving results on the ground.
AI-powered combat simulations also play a fundamental role in armed forces training. These systems are capable of recreating realistic war environments, where hundreds, if not thousands, of variables can be simulated in real time. Thanks to AI, it is possible to model complex scenarios, test different strategies and simulate the consequences of failure or success. These simulations are not just limited to static scenarios, but can incorporate the adaptability of enemy forces, which adjust their tactics according to the actions of the player or simulated entity. For example, armies can practise defence strategies against surprise attacks, ambushes or guerrilla-style assaults, while incorporating scenarios for cyber attacks, electronic warfare or asymmetric warfare. Thanks to enhanced learning algorithms, these simulations are constantly being improved, enabling military forces to test a multitude of situations and optimise their reactions in a controlled environment.
Another area where AI is playing an increasingly crucial role is the optimisation of resource management in wartime. Armed forces have to manage a wide range of resources, from munitions and vehicles to logistics and manpower. By using AI to analyse requirements in real time and forecast demand, commanders can avoid critical shortages and adjust the allocation of resources according to the involution of operations on the ground. For example, AI can estimate when a stock of ammunition is about to run out and recommend the reorganisation of supply leagues. It can also anticipate the need for fuel or spare parts for military vehicles, reducing the risk of breakdowns and interruptions to operations.
The integration of AI into military planning is not only an asset for the great powers, but also enables less well-equipped armies to improve their planning and capabilities. By providing advanced

analytical tools and accessible simulations, AI is levelling the playing field between nations and enabling smaller or less technologically advanced armies to draw on the same kinds of strategic information and forecasts as the military forces of more powerful countries. This could have a considerable impact on the balance forces in regions where limited resources are often compensated for by more refined strategic planning.

However, the introduction of AI into military planning also raises ethical and strategic questions. While AI can optimise resource management and improve the accuracy of decisions, there is an inherent danger of over-reliance on these systems. One of the major challenges is to ensure that AI remains a decision support tool, rather than a complete substitute for human skills in military strategy. Indeed, despite all the computing power of AI algorithms, war remains a profoundly human phenomenon, requiring decisions to be taken on the basis of values, morals and politics. Military commanders must therefore continue to play a central role, overseeing the recommendations generated by the AI and incorporating elements of human judgement that are beyond the AI's ability to analyse, such as political considerations and the long-term implications of certain actions.

One of the most controversial aspects of the application of artificial intelligence (AI) in the military field is undoubtedly the development of **lethal autonomous weapon systems (SALA).** These weapons represent a fundamental break with traditional military technologies, as they require no direct human intervention to select and engage targets. Unlike drone or guided missile systems, which still depend on human supervision to validate strikes, SALAs are capable of operating autonomously by analysing their environment, identifying targets and deciding what action to take, all without the intervention of a human operator on the ground. This marks a radical change in the way military conflicts can be conducted in the future.

The development of these systems relies on advanced algorithms, often based on machine learning and computer vision, which enable SALA to analyse images in real time and make decisions on the basis of well-defined criteria. These criteria can include an individual's posture, the type of equipment they are wearing, or even the heat signature of their body or vehicles. By combining this data with additional contextual information, AI enables ALS systems to detect potential threats with an accuracy that often exceeds that of a human operator. This makes these systems particularly effective for large-scale military operations, where the ability to process and react quickly to large volumes of information is essential.

One of the best-known and most controversial examples of the use of these systems in real conflicts is the incident involving the Kargu-2 autonomous drone, a tactical combat drone that was allegedly used in 2020 during fighting in Libya. This drone, developed by Turkish company STM, is said to have acted autonomously, identifying and attacking targets without direct human intervention. According to reports, the Kargu-2 was able to attack fighters in the Tripoli area, acting completely independently after being launched on a mission, without human operators having to validate each strike. Although the Turkish government has played down this information, the case has been the subject of worldwide debate, raising concerns about the control and responsibility associated with the use of autonomous weapons in warfare.

The deployment of the Kargu-2 in Libya marked a worrying step in the development of these technologies. Although the incident was relatively limited, it showed that SALAs can be used in real-life armed conflict contexts, and have the potential to be a major transformation in the way combat may be conducted in the future.

If other countries, such as the United States, Russia and China, also invest in similar technologies, the scale of the phenomenon is likely to grow exponentially in the coming years. In the United States, for example, projects involving autonomous military robots are already underway, notably as part of the war against drones, with prototypes being developed by the Pentagon. In Russia, autonomous weapons systems are also being developed to enhance the effectiveness of the armed forces, particularly in the area of precision strikes.

However, the deployment of such systems raises major ethical and legal issues. One of the main arguments against SALAs is the fear of losing human control over life-and-death decisions. In a military context, the risk is that these weapons could attack civilian targets, make targeting errors or even be hacked and used against non-legitimate objectives. Supporters of human control over autonomous lethal weapons argue that machines, while effective in terms of speed and accuracy, lack the moral judgement that is essential for applying the principles of international humanitarian law, such as the distinction between combatants and civilians and the proportionality of attacks.

In addition, the risk of autonomous weaponry raises questions about responsibility. Who is responsible when autonomous weapons make a mistake, killing innocent people or violating international law? States that develop these weapons may find themselves in a delicate situation, where it is difficult for them to attribute responsibility in the event of a violation of the laws of war, particularly if the action was taken entirely autonomously by the machine. Discussions on the regulation and rules of engagement for SALA have therefore become a priority for international organisations such as the UN and the Organisation for the Prohibition of Chemical Weapons (OPCW).

Although SALA can offer undeniable strategic advantages,

particularly in terms of speed action, reduced risks for soldiers and increased precision, they raise major challenges in terms of control, ethics and international law. Their rapid development in certain countries highlights the urgent need for clear international regulations to govern the use of such technologies. The world will have to navigate between technological innovation and humanitarian imperatives to avoid an uncontrolled escalation of conflicts.

where machines can potentially make life and death decisions without any human intervention.

The use of SALA is the subject of lively ethical and legal debate within the international community. Some believe that these systems reduce the risks to soldiers and enable strikes to be carried out with greater precision, thereby limiting collateral damage. Others, however, are concerned about the moral implications and the risk of dehumanising conflicts, where life and death decisions are taken by machines. The absence of direct human control also raises questions about responsibility in the event of error, blunder or illegitimate attack. Many human rights , as well as experts in international law, are calling for strict regulation or even a ban on these autonomous weapons before they become the norm on the battlefield.

Alongside the development of autonomous lethal weapons systems, artificial intelligence (AI) is also playing an increasingly central role in **military cyber security.** With the rise in cyber attacks and the constant evolution of digital threats, modern armies are turning to AI to protect their critical infrastructures and communications networks. In a world where war is no longer confined to physical battlefields, military cyber security has become a key element of national defence strategy.

Cyber security is a particularly vulnerable area, as cyber attacks can not only paralyse vital systems but also compromise sensitive information. Cyber threats are diverse and include attempted intrusions into military networks, *ransomware* attacks, attempts to sabotage command and control systems, and disinformation campaigns aimed at confusing the armed forces or the government. These attacks are often carried out by adversaries using increasingly sophisticated techniques, rendering old defence methods obsolete. In this context, AI offers innovative solutions capable of spotting intrusions and reacting more quickly than humans, guaranteeing better protection for sensitive networks.

One of the great advantages of AI in cybersecurity is its ability to detect anomalies in real time. Unlike traditional systems that rely on previously identified threat signatures, AI is able to learn from large amounts of data to detect anomalous behaviour, even that which has not yet been observed. Using machine learning algorithms, AI systems can analyse millions of transactions or communications in a matter of seconds, identifying suspicious patterns that may signal an attempted intrusion or a cyber attack in corns. In other words, AI makes it possible to detect unknown attacks or new forms of threat, which is essential given the rapidity of involution of cybercriminals and state hackers.

Countries such as the United States, China and Israel are investing massively in AI technologies to improve the cybersecurity of their military infrastructures. In the US, the Department of Defense has established initiatives such as the AI and Cybersecurity Initiative, which aims to integrate AI capabilities into all aspects of military cybersecurity, from attack detection to incident response. This initiative includes efforts to improve predictive threat analysis capabilities and strengthen the resilience of military networks. The aim is to make military networks not only more secure, but also more adaptable in the face of an ever-changing digital landscape.

Israel, renowned for its cybersecurity capabilities, has also integrated AI into the defence of its military networks. As one of the world leaders in defence technologies, Israel is using AI to strengthen the security of its critical infrastructures, particularly in the context of geopolitical tensions with its neighbours. The country relies on AI systems to constantly monitor the activity of its military networks and detect any attempted intrusion before it can cause any damage. In 2020the Israeli government introduced measures improve the cyber security of its army by using AI technologies capable of adapting to emerging threats.

One of the major challenges of integrating AI into military cyber security lies in the risk of flaws in the systems themselves. Although AI is capable of enhancing security, it can also be vulnerable to attack, like any other digital system. If adversaries manage to manipulate or hack an AI system, this can have serious consequences for the security of military networks. In addition, the complexity of AI and their ability to evolve over time make them difficult to monitor. Cybersecurity managers must therefore constantly update their models and ensure continuous monitoring to any flaws or manipulation in the system.

Finally, AI also offers benefits in terms of the resilience of critical infrastructures. In the event of a cyber attack, military systems can use AI to quickly redirect resources to backup networks or reorganise priorities to maintain the effectiveness of operations. This reduces the risk of disruption to military operations, ensuring that armed forces can continue to function even in the event of a major crisis. This increased resilience is essential for maintaining strategic superiority on the ground, particularly in times of war or intense confrontation.

In short, AI in military cybersecurity represents a major advance in the protection of critical infrastructures and communications networks. Thanks to its ability to detect, analyse and respond in real time, AI enables armed forces to defend themselves against increasingly sophisticated cyber attacks and protect military operations from digital threats. However, its use raises challenges, particularly in terms of the security of the AI systems themselves and human control over automated processes. In the face of these challenges, international cooperation and the development of safety standards are essential to ensure that the benefits of AI in the military domain are maximised while minimising the associated risks.

Artificial intelligence (AI) is playing a growing role in **the transformation of military equipment logistics and maintenance,** offering innovative solutions that are revolutionising the way armed forces manage their equipment and ensure its operational readiness. In particular, AI-based predictive management systems are enabling to anticipate maintenance requirements, optimise equipment lifespan and reduce maintenance costs. These technological advances help to maintain armies in a state of maximum availability, while ensuring greater efficiency in the management of resources.

One of the main advantages of AI in this field is its ability to analyse large quantities of data collected from different military systems and equipment, such as armoured vehicles, aircraft, ships and submarines. This data can include information on equipment use, real-time sensor data, performance indicators and maintenance histories. Using machine learning algorithms, AI is able to identify patterns that often escape human observation, enabling anomalies, abnormal wear or potential failures to be detected before actually occur. For example, by analysing engine vibration, component temperature or oil pressure, an AI-powered system can predict that an engine is likely to fail in the short term, enabling repairs to be carried out before the equipment becomes unusable in the field.

The financial benefits are also considerable. Predictive

maintenance makes it possible to reduce the costs associated with costly emergency repairs and prolonged equipment downtime, while maximising the lifespan of equipment. By detecting potential failures at an early stage, AI enables armed forces to plan repairs strategically, avoiding excessive expenditure associated with serious breakdowns that can lead to extended repair times. This is particularly relevant in a context where defence budgets are often constrained and effective resource management is essential.

Let's take the example of military aircraft management. Modern air forces depend on a large number of fighter, transport and surveillance aircraft, which are subject to intense operating conditions and require regular maintenance to ensure they are in good working order. Thanks to AI, sensors built into aircraft can collect data in real time, such as engine temperature, fuel levels, the state of hydraulic systems and much more. This data is then transmitted to AI systems that analyse it to identify early warning signs of faults, such as an imbalance in tyre pressure, unusual lubricant levels or components that are wearing beyond normal levels. As a result, maintenance technicians can plan repairs before a breakdown occurs, reducing aircraft downtime and ensuring that the aircraft is operational when needed.

Similarly, in the naval sector, large warships, aircraft carriers and submarines are complex and expensive pieces of equipment, requiring regular maintenance to ensure they run smoothly. IA systems can analyse a multitude of data from sensors installed on the ship's various systems, such as engines, electrical generators, cooling or propulsion systems. AI can unusual fluctuations in these systems and trigger alerts to warn maintenance teams. The use of this technology makes it possible to better plan maintenance cycles and intervene in the event of a failure before it affects the ship's mission capabilities, while reducing the need have constant maintenance personnel on board for manual inspections.

Artificial intelligence also plays a major role in optimising training and simulations. Armies around the world use AI-based simulators to train their personnel in equipment maintenance management. These simulations enable technicians to learn how to detect signs of failure in a virtual environment before being confronted with real-life situations. This ongoing training improves the skills and responsiveness of maintenance staff, which translates into better equipment performance in the field. AI can also be used to create more realistic simulation environments, incorporating complex fault scenarios to test the resilience of systems and the ability of teams to respond to emergencies.

AI is also helping to improve the overall management of military equipment fleets, whether armoured vehicles, ships or aircraft. By means of integrated management systems, AI makes it possible to monitor in real time the condition of each piece of equipment, the frequency of maintenance and the associated costs. This approach not only optimises the use of equipment, but also enables informed decisions to be made replacing or upgrading equipment, based on its overall condition and maintenance costs.

Artificial intelligence (AI) is playing an increasingly central role in **military intelligence operations,** transforming the way intelligence agencies collect, analyse and exploit information. AI offers unrivalled analytical capabilities, making it possible to immense volumes of data from diverse and often unstructured sources. It plays an essential role in potential threats, identifying trends and anticipating events, offering a crucial strategic advantage in modern conflicts.

One of the main strengths of AI in military intelligence lies in its ability to process and analyse data on a scale and with a speed that would be impossible for human analysts. The sources of data available to military intelligence are varied and abundant: intercepted communications, satellite images, radio transmissions, data from sensors deployed in the field, but also information from social networks, blogs or online forums. The amount of data produced every day is such that it is virtually impossible for human agents to sort and analyse all this content effectively in real time. AI, on the other hand, is capable of tackling this volume of data systematically, automatically and quickly, by applying sophisticated machine learning, semantic analysis and image recognition algorithms.

Satellite image analysis is another area in which AI has profoundly transformed military intelligence capabilities. Satellites provide high-resolution images of strategic geographical areas, but the amount of visual data they generate is immense. Manual analysis of these images would not only be time-consuming but also prone to human error. Thanks to AI, systems can not only analyse thousands of images in a few hours, but also detect specific objects, such as military vehicles, secret bases or missile launch facilities. The AI uses deep neural networks to recognise specific patterns in satellite images, identifying changes in infrastructure, the disposition of troops, or movements of military equipment. For example, if an army suddenly moves a large number of vehicles into a normally quiet area, the AI can detect this quickly and alert intelligence analysts, enabling them to better anticipate opposing movements and adjust strategies accordingly .

AI is also used to detect potential threats before materialise. Using predictive analysis systems, it can model different war or crisis scenarios based on available data and anticipate enemy actions. This enables intelligence managers to make informed decisions about military readiness, troop deployment and strategic priorities.

For example, an AI system can analyse the movements of an armed group over several months, studying their habits and trajectories, to predict where they might attack next. These anticipatory enhance the responsiveness of intelligence services and increase the chances of intervening effectively before hostile actions come to fruition.

Another field in which AI plays a key role is the surveillance of sensitive areas. For example, in regions at war or under stress, autonomous drones equipped with sensors and image analysis algorithms can constantly monitor specific areas. These drones can carry out prolonged reconnaissance missions without human intervention, detecting changes in terrain, troop movements or hidden enemy installations. AI thus provide constant surveillance, even in high-risk or difficult-to-access areas.

Artificial intelligence (AI) plays a central role in military intelligence operations, and several recent examples illustrate how this technology is being deployed in the field to improve decision-making and anticipate threats.

One of the most notable examples of use of AI in military intelligence is the use of drones for data collection and analysis. One example is the MQ-9 Reaper drone used by the US army. This drone, which is equipped sophisticated sensors, can carry out extended reconnaissance of a given area by capturing high-resolution images and analysing them in real time using AI. AI helps to identify specific features on the ground, such as groups of military vehicles or missile launch facilities. In 2017, an MQ-9 Reaper detected and tracked a convoy of Islamic State (IS) fighters in Syria, enabling US forces to precisely target the convoy, reducing the risk of civilian casualties. AI enabled this data to be analysed quickly and efficiently, filtering information to focus only on potential threats.

AI is also used to analyse satellite images. For example, the private company Maxar Technologies uses AI technologies to analyse satellite images taken by commercial satellites in order to identify military activities in sensitive geographical areas. During the growing tensions in the South China Sea, the authorities used satellite images to track the construction of new military bases by China on artificial lees. AI was used analyse these images to detect changes in the construction of military installations and the movement of ships and equipment, providing analysts with crucial information in real time. AI systems not only help to interpret these images, but also to predict future movements based on historical patterns, enabling Chinese actions to be anticipated.

Another example is the use of AI by the Israeli army to monitor the borders with Gaza. Israel has drones and ground sensors equipped with AI algorithms to monitor the movements of Palestinian militants. These systems can identify threats by analysing subtle variations in behaviour, such as a change in the trajectory of vehicles or unusual gatherings of individuals. In 2018, an Israeli drone equipped with AI technology intercepted missiles from Gaza, using its image recognition system to distinguish missiles from harmless objects. These autonomous AI systems enable the Israeli forces to rapidly detect attacks or attempted intrusions, boosting their ability to react more quickly.

During the recent tensions between the United States and Iran, AI was used to monitor Iranian activities in the Persian Gulf region. In 2019, an incident involving a British oil tanker was attributed to Iranian attacks. AI was deployed to monitor the movements of Iranian ships in the Strait of Hormuz, using satellite imagery and positioning data to identify suspicious manoeuvres. Thanks to ГIA, military analysts were able to observe concentrations of ships and predict potential attacks before they happened.

As part of the war in Ukraine, ГIA has been used for visual intelligence analysis in war zones. The Ukrainian army uses ГIApowered drones to monitor Russian positions, enemy tanks or armoured vehicles and transmit this information instantly to ground forces. Similarly, ΓIA helps images from videos taken by drones or satellites to spot troop movements and assess the risk of attack. These systems enable decisions to be made in real time, reducing human error and increasing the effectiveness of weaponry.

One of the fundamental aspects of human intelligence lies in the individual's ability to interpret information in a specific context. AI can process raw data, such as satellite images, intercepted conversations or publications on social networks, but it does not have the capacity to fully understand the human context of this information. For example, a sentence overheard an intercepted conversation can have a completely different meaning depending on the relationships between the individuals who uttered it, the social or political environment in which it uttered, or the non-verbalised intentions behind the words. Human agents, on the other hand, are able to grasp these subtle nuances, enabling them to make more nuanced and more reliable analyses.

Another key element of human intelligence is the ability to understand the motivations and strategies of adversaries. AI, however sophisticated, does not have the capacity to grasp the psychology of a group, its internal dynamics or its long-term strategies. For example, in complex conflicts where non-state actors, such as terrorist groups or insurgents, are involved, it is essential to understand their ideologies, objectives and command structure. Although ΓIA can spot patterns and perform statistical analysis from available data, it lacks the empathy, intuition and human understanding needed to grasp the subtleties of these groups, their deep motivations and worldview. These elements are often key to anticipating the next steps in a conflict and developing effective strategies.

Human intelligence is also irreplaceable when it comes to decision-making in ambiguous or uncertain situations. In times of war, the information available is often fragmented and can be contradictory. AI can analyse data and make predictions on the basis of models and algorithms, but final decisions, especially in critical situations, must sometimes be based on human judgements that take account of factors that ΓIA cannot always incorporate, such as ethics, international law or sensitive political considerations. For example, when information about potential targets is available, it may be necessary to take into account human factors such as the impact on the civilian population, the effects of a strike on regional stability or the international diplomatic response. These decisions, which are crucial in the conduct of military operations, require a more complex understanding than a machine can provide.

In addition, human intelligence remains essential for building trust and relationships in complex environments. Human intelligence officers are often able to develop networks of contacts in sensitive areas, interact with informatene and gather information directly on the ground. This type of intelligence, known as "HUMINT" (Human Intelligence), is based on direct human interaction and on information that cannot be gathered by automated systems. Spies or agents infiltrating an enemy group can obtain strategic information, establish relationships of trust with local informants or understand internal dynamics that sensors or satellites cannot perceive. The ability to negotiate, manipulate or interrogate people to extract information remains a key human skill that is still at the heart of intelligence missions.

Finally, a major aspect that ΓIA can never replace is the ability to react to unexpected or unique situations. Military conflicts are often marked by unexpected events, rapid changes in the situation or innovative tactics employed by the adversary. In such circumstances, the human instinct and personal experience of an intelligence analyst, who can demonstrate creativity and flexibility in solving new problems, are irreplaceable assets. AI, which operates mainly on the basis of past data and pre-programmed scenarios, may find it difficult to adapt to these unforeseen circumstances, as it lacks the capacity to innovate in the same way as a human being.

The integration of artificial intelligence (AI) in the military field marks a true technological revolution, affecting not only combat techniques and defence strategies, but also the way in which nations approach war and international security. By making it easier **to automate certain tasks and increasing analysis and decision-making capabilities,** AI brings considerable benefits. In particular, it improves the effectiveness of military operations, increases the precision of strikes, reduces the loss of human lives and promotes better management of resources. However, these advantages are not without raising profound ethical and legal questions, which in turn fuel a complex debate on the regulation and control these technologies.

At the same time, AI is transforming military logistics, improving resource management, predictive equipment maintenance and supply planning. Armed forces can now better anticipate their needs, manage stocks of ammunition, fuel and other essential materials more effectively, and even plan repairs and maintenance on vehicles and aircraft before they break down. This optimised management not only reduces costs, but also improves the operational availability of equipment. Thanks to AI, armies can prepare for any eventuality, ensuring that their forces remain ready to intervene at all times.

Despite these advantages, ΓIA in the military field raises crucial ethical and legal questions. One of the most worrying debates concerns the question of liability in the event of error or collateral

damage caused by autonomous weapons systems. In a conflict, the use of technologies that make autonomous decisions - notably autonomous lethal weapons - can lead to situations where it becomes difficult to determine who is responsible for the actions of a machine. If an autonomous drone mistakenly engages a target and kills civilians, who should take responsibility? The AI manufacturer, the military commander who authorised the attack, or the state itself? Such questions not only complicate the principles liability, they also pose complex legal challenges.
As well as questions of accountability, there are also concerns about transparency and . Military AI systems are often perceived as "black boxes", whose decision-making process is opaque, even to the humans who supervise them. If the AI makes a decision autonomously, how can it be guaranteed that this decision complies with international humanitarian law, which prohibits attacks on civilians or non-military targets? In addition, there y concerns about the possibility of AI systems being manipulated or hacked. In a military context, where information is extremely sensitive, the possibility of a malicious actor managing to hijack an autonomous weapons system or falsify intelligence data feeding an algorithm is a real risk. Vulnerabilities in AI systems can compromise not only a country's military operations, but also its national security.
Added to this is the problem of the dehumanisation of conflicts. Autonomous weapons, sometimes referred to as "killer robots", are seen by some as a potential threat to the human condition in armed conflict. Critics argue that entrusting machines with the power to make life-or-death decisions removes the human aspect from warfare, reducing the moral responsibility of the decisions taken. Such a development could lead to the uncontrolled escalation of conflicts, where military decisions are dictated by algorithms, without the moderation that human reflection can

provide. This could, for example, lead to more frequent and more destructive wars, as leaders may be tempted to use autonomous weapons without being fully aware of the human consequences.
This race for innovation is also fuelled by the need to maintain a strategic balance on a global scale. In a world where the major powers are vying for technological hegemony, every advance in military AI represents a major strategic lever. Developed countries are investing billions of dollars in cutting-edge research, not only to strengthen their military capacity, but also to prevent potential adversaries from gaining a decisive technological advantage. However, this race also has geopolitical consequences, as it raises concerns about the proliferation of these technologies to authoritarian regimes or non-state groups, who may make irresponsible or immoral use of them.

CHAPTER 2

The limits to the use of artificial intelligence in the military field

One of the major challenges facing artificial intelligence in the military field is its **dependence on data.** For an AI system to work effectively, it needs to be fed massive amounts of data, from multiple sources such as satellites, drones, sensors deployed in the field, as well as strategic databases. This data is essential for AI to be able to carry out analyses, make decisions and perform specific tasks, whether they involve reconnaissance, targeting, logistics or surveillance. But this dependence on data, while largely an asset, can also prove to be a considerable weakness, because the quality, reliability and accuracy of the data are crucial to the success of the mission.

In a military environment, data collection and analysis are not as straightforward as in other sectors. Conditions on the ground, often hostile and unpredictable, can disrupt this process. Electromagnetic interference is one of the main sources of disruption. In warfare, the use of jammers and devices designed to interfere with communication signals is commonplace. This interference can affect the transmission of essential data, whether from drones, satellites or even ground-based communications systems. A sensor installed on a drone, for example, can be disconnected or disrupted by a jamming attack, compromising the quality of information it transmits to the AI. If the AI is unable to obtain reliable information, its ability to make informed decisions becomes severely impaired, leading to costly and sometimes catastrophic errors.

Another source of disruption to data quality in a military context is related to sensor failures. These sensors, which may be on-board devices on UAVs, satellites or vehicles, are susceptible to technical failures due to wear and tear, tampering with the equipment or even external attacks. For example, a faulty optical sensor on a drone may not be able to distinguish correctly between different targets on a battlefield. This means that the AI, which relies on this data to identify threats, may come to erroneous conclusions, such as incorrect identification of an enemy or a civilian. If these errors are not corrected in time, they can lead to misdirected strikes, damage to non-military infrastructure or, worse still, the loss of innocent civilian lives.

Furthermore, in a complex war environment, it is possible for the data collected to be erroneous or misinterpreted. Information can come from multiple sources, sometimes contradictory, and AI can struggle to analyse it correctly if the underlying algorithms are not sophisticated enough to understand the nuances of the situation. For example, data transmitted by a reconnaissance drone may indicate the presence of enemy soldiers in a given area, but erroneous information or misinterpretation of the context may lead the AI to make a premature decision. What's more, human failings in the analysis of the data can contribute to a misinterpretation of the information, which can have serious repercussions on the strategy deployed on the ground.

Another difficulty lies in managing the huge amount of data generated. AI systems need to process huge volumes of information from a variety of sources in real time . However, this implies not only the ability to collect and store this data, but also to guarantee its quality and relevance at the time it is needed. Another challenge lies in filtering this data. Many types of information, whether digital or human, can be superfluous or even harmful, particularly if they are biased or manipulated. AI must be able to sort through all this information and focus on what is relevant. For example, if a military intelligence system uses social network data to identify potential threats, it pent be confronted with manipulated information, rumours or propaganda that distorts the conclusions. Poorly trained IA or poorly managed data can amplify incorrect information and lead to an inappropriate response.

Protection against misinformation and data manipulation is therefore becoming a crucial issue. In the military context, data can be deliberately altered by adversaries with the aim of disrupting the decision-making process. Cyber attacks aimed at manipulating or falsifying information sent to AI systems can seriously compromise military missions. These attacks can range from the introduction of false signals or information into databases to more sophisticated attempts to manipulate the analysis carried out by the AI itself. In the event of a successful attack, an autonomous weapons system, for example, could be led to engage a target that does not represent a real threat, or worse still, fail to react to an imminent threat. So data security is as important as the quality of the data itself, and rigorous cyber-security measures are needed to protect military AI systems from malicious cyber-attacks.

Because of these challenges, the reliability of military AI relies on strict control protocols, rigorous data management and constant human monitoring. Although AI can provide powerful tools for analysing war situations, it remains dependent on the environment and the accuracy of information it receives. An AI system without human intervention, or poorly fed with inaccurate or biased data, can quickly become ineffective and even dangerous. This vulnerability linked to data quality is fuelling the debate on the limits of automation in military conflicts, and raises the question of whether confidence in machines to make critical decisions in the field can be truly justified.

One of the major concerns associated with the use of artificial intelligence in the military domain, particularly in autonomous weapons systems, is the **vulnerabilities associated with hacking.**

The cyber threat is becoming increasingly sophisticated, and the possibility that malicious actors will manage to hijack or manipulate military AI systems raises considerable risks. If an autonomous weapons system is compromised by hacking, the consequences can be dramatic. Indeed, a tei hijacking would not be limited to the impact on a single military mission, but could have large-scale destabilising effects, jeopardising national security, allies and even sensitive civilian infrastructures.

One of the most worrying scenarios would be where a defence AI system is hacked and used against the interests of the state that developed it. For example, an autonomous military drone system or defence robot could, once manipulated, be directed against strategic installations such as military bases, critical infrastructures or even civilians. A malicious actor could exploit a security flaw in the AI system to redirect weaponry to unintended targets, thereby compromising valuable human and material resources. The AI, unable to discern the origin of the attack or the legitimacy of the orders, would indiscriminately follow erroneous or malicious instructions, producing potentially catastrophic results.

Another risk is the possibility of a terrorist attack using a hacked autonomous weapon system. Terrorist groups or hostile actors may turn to advanced technologies such as AI to carry out targeted attacks. If an AI-powered military drone system were hacked and diverted from its original functions, it could be used to attack civilian areas or critical infrastructure, such power stations, transport networks or hospitals. This kind of attack can cause massive loss of life and considerable damage, while profoundly destabilising a country's security. The consequences of such a misuse of AI in a terrorist act, in addition to the physical damage, would include a loss of confidence in modern defence systems and widespread fear the exploitation of military technologies by

invisible enemies.
One of the major challenges is that, unlike traditional weaponry, AI systems are extremely complex and often depend on interconnections between several platforms, such as drones, satellites and ground control stations. Each link in this chain presents a point of vulnerability. If a hacker manages to penetrate one of these systems, he can full access to the autonomous weapons capabilities deployed. This interconnection also makes the system even more susceptible to Denial of Service (DDoS) attacks, where a massive flow of data requests overloads a system and renders it unusable, disrupting military operations.
What's more, the rapid evolution of electronic warfare technologies further complicates the task of securing military AI systems. Electronic warfare, which consists of disrupting, intercepting or manipulating electronic communications, includes the possibility of jamming signals sent to autonomous weapons systems. For example, a command signal intended for an autonomous drone can be intercepted and manipulated, or a GPS signal can be distorted to take the drone to the wrong destination. Jamming attacks, combined with vulnerabilities in the IA's coding or decision-making process, can lead to major failures.
One of the most serious consequences of this situation is that governments and their armed forces may lose control over technologies that they have developed and deployed for strategic purposes. Managing military AI therefore requires not only sophisticated detection and intrusion prevention capabilities, but also redundancy and backup protocols. The military will need to design systems capable of withstanding cyber-attacks while maintaining sufficient human control to ensure that critical decisions are not taken incorrectly or manipulated by a hacker.
Faced with this threat, it is becoming imperative for governments to strengthen IT protection around the AI systems used in military

operations. This means investing heavily in encryption technologies, secure communication protocols and increasingly sophisticated means of detecting cyber intrusions. Governments must also set up specialised teams cybersecurity experts to constantly test and audit military AI systems, in order to prevent security breaches .

One of the major concerns associated with the use of artificial intelligence in the military domain, particularly in autonomous weapons systems, is the **vulnerabilities associated with hacking.** The cyberthreat is becoming increasingly sophisticated, and the possibility that malicious actors could manage to hijack or manipulate military AI systems raises considerable risks. If an autonomous weapons system is compromised by hacking, the consequences can be dramatic. Indeed, such a hijacking would not be limited to the impact on a single military mission, but could have destabilising effects on a large scale, jeopardising national security, allies and even sensitive civilian infrastructures.

One of the most worrying scenarios is when a defence AI system is hacked and used against the interests of the state that developed it. For example, an autonomous military drone system or defence robot could, once manipulated, be directed against strategic installations such as military bases, critical infrastructures or even civilians. A malicious actor could exploit a security flaw in the AI system to redirect weaponry to unintended targets, thereby compromising valuable human and material resources. The AI, unable to discern the origin of the attack or the legitimacy of the orders, would indiscriminately follow erroneous or malicious instructions, producing potentially catastrophic results.

Another risk is the possibility of a terrorist attack using a hacked autonomous weapons system. Terrorist groups or hostile actors may turn to advanced technologies such as AI to carry out targeted attacks. If a military drone system equipped with AI is hacked and diverted from its original functions, it could be used to attack civilian areas or critical infrastructure, such as power stations, transport networks or hospitals. This type of attack can cause massive loss of life and considerable damage, while profoundly destabilising a country's security. The consequences of such a misuse of AI in a terrorist act, in addition to the physical damage, would include a loss of confidence in modern defence systems and widespread fear of military technologies being exploited by invisible enemies.

What's more, the rapid development of electronic warfare technologies makes it even more difficult to secure military AI systems. Electronic warfare, which consists of disrupting, intercepting or manipulating electronic communications, includes the possibility of jamming signals sent to autonomous weapons systems. For example, a command signal intended for an autonomous drone can be intercepted and manipulated, or a GPS signal can be distorted to take the drone to the wrong destination. Jamming attacks, combined with vulnerabilities in the IA's coding or decision-making process, can lead to major failures.

One of the most serious consequences of this situation is that governments and their armed forces may lose control over technologies that they have developed and deployed for strategic purposes. Managing military AI therefore requires not only sophisticated intrusion detection and prevention capabilities, but also redundancy and backup protocols. Militaries need to design systems that can withstand cyber-attacks while maintaining sufficient human control to ensure that critical decisions are not taken incorrectly or manipulated by a hacker.

In addition to direct attacks on autonomous weapons systems, another area of vulnerability concerns connected military infrastructures. AI is used not only for defence systems, but also for managing communications networks, logistics and military intelligence. The cybersecurity of these networks is therefore becoming a fundamental strategic issue. A successful attack against artificial intelligence systems managing military databases or communications networks could paralyse an entire army. The loss of crucial data, the compromise of communication channels between military units or the manipulation of intelligence reports can have dramatic consequences for national and international security.

In the face of this threat, it is becoming imperative for governments to strengthen IT protection around the AI systems used in military operations. This means investing heavily in encryption technologies, secure communication protocols and increasingly sophisticated means of detecting cyber intrusions. Governments also need to set up specialised teams of cyber security experts to continuously test and audit military AI systems to prevent security .

The issue of responsibility in military AI is one of the most complex and controversial, largely due to the lack of transparency of artificial intelligence systems, which are often compared to "black boxes". These systems, whether autonomous drones, combat robots or autonomous weapons systems, are based on extremely sophisticated algorithms that can make autonomous decisions based on thousands of pieces of data in real time. However, these algorithms are not always easily understood by humans, which raises a number of ethical, legal and practical questions.

The lack of transparency in AI systems makes it difficult to understand the decision-making process behind them. Indeed, whereas a human operator can justify his actions by explaining his logic and decisions on the basis of his judgement, an IA often only provides a solution without a clear explanation of how it arrived at this conclusion. This opacity creates a significant barrier when it comes to tracing a decision, particularly in a military operation where human lives are at stake. An AI's decision to target a military installation, an enemy force or, in more worrying cases, innocent civilians, can seem arbitrary and difficult to justify.

This lack of transparency is accompanied by an inability to provide a clear and precise answer to the question of legal responsibility when an error occurs. If a system

autonomous weapon makes a targeting error, by hitting a civilian target for example, it becomes very complex to point the finger of blame. Should the engineer who designed the AI algorithm be held responsible? The military officer who deployed the system? Or the machine itself, which seems illogical given that it has no conscience or intention? The absence of clear human oversight or a well-defined chain of responsibility further complicates this dilemma. Without the ability trace the AI's decisions, it is virtually impossible to know who, if anyone, should be held responsible for an inappropriate action. This poses major legal problems, particularly with regard to compliance with international humanitarian law, the Geneva Conventions and other international standards relating to war.

The proportionality of an attack is a fundamental principle of the law of war that raises questions in the context of military IA. This principle states that military action must not cause suffering that is excessive in relation to the military advantage sought. When an AI makes an attack decision, it may be programmed to maximise effectiveness based on the available data, but it may not be able to measure the proportionality of its actions in the same nuanced way as an experienced human commander. For example, an attack on a strategically important target may result in considerable civilian casualties, but the machine, due to its lack of contextual and moral judgement, may not perceive this imbalance. In the absence of an accountability framework and the ability to trace decisions, AI can be used to justify disproportionate attacks and violate the principles just war.

This lack of transparency and understanding of the AI decision-making process is therefore a major obstacle to the control and regulation of autonomous weapons systems. It becomes extremely difficult to verify whether these systems comply with the norms and principles of international humanitarian law. Without a clear vision of how decisions are taken by AI, it is virtually impossible to ensure that military actions carried out by these technologies comply with the laws of war. This makes controlling the use of force particularly complex. The lack of direct human supervision and the difficulty of auditing IA decision-making processes may lead to a situation where acts of war are conducted by systems whose actions cannot be fully explained, calling into question the legitimacy of decisions and the use of force.

In this context, the issue of accountability becomes paramount. There is an urgent need to develop mechanisms for monitoring, auditing and understanding the decisions made by AI systems in a military setting. This requires specific regiementations, rigorous ethical principles and transparency protocols that ensure that, even in an environment where ΓIA is used for autonomous decision-making, the accountability and legality of actions remain clear and tractable. Governments, international institutions and ethics experts must work together to design rules adapted to these new technological realities, so as to avoid abuse and ensure compliance with human rights and international law.

Artificial intelligence, with its ability analyse immense volumes of data and model complex scenarios, offers revolutionary potential in many fields, y including the military sector. However, this same power raises major concerns due **to algorithmic biases,** which can affect the reliability and justice of decisions made by

AI systems. Algorithmic biases refer to systematic patterns in the results generated by an AI system, which often result from the data used to train these systems. These biases, although sometimes invisible or subtle in the process, can have devastating effects, particularly in a context as critical as that of military operations, where the slightest error of judgement can have tragic human consequences.

AI systems are trained on historical data, which inherently reflects the biases, errors and inequalities that exist in the real world. If the data used to train an IA comes from biased sources or is insufficiently diverse they risk incorporating these same biases into their decision-making processes. For example, an AI system designed to analyse the behaviour of enemy forces pent be trained on historical data that is already marked by inaccurate or stereotyped representations of certain geographical regions or ethnic groups. In this case, ГIA pent misinterpret information and target individuals or groups based on characteristics that are irrelevant to the actual threat they represent. This can lead to unjustified attacks on civilians or non-military areas, causing unnecessary loss of life and exacerbating existing tensions.

The impact of algorithmic biases is not limited simply to errors in target recognition or distorted threat assessments. These biases can also alter the way military resources are allocated, affecting the prioritisation of operations and the distribution of manpower. For example, if an algorithm is biased in its analysis of geopolitical data, it may recommend military engagement against a target perceived as more threatening on the basis of erroneous criteria, while neglecting greater risks elsewhere. This can lead to protracted conflicts or to an excessive concentration of military efforts on targets that are not really strategic, despite other more pressing threats.

In the military context, one of the major challenges is that these errors are not always easy to detect. AI systems, especially those based on deep neural networks, are often described as "black boxes" because of their lack of transparency. Even if an algorithmic bias exists in the system, it can be difficult to identify or understand without an in-depth analysis of the training data and the inner workings of the algorithm. In addition, the speed with which these systems make decisions, particularly in real-time combat situations, makes it even more difficult for humans to intervene to correct errors. In this context, a misinterpretation of data by ΓIA can have irreversible consequences before a human operator even has a chance react.

What's more, in war situations where information is often incomplete, ambiguous or constantly changing, AI can be led to make decisions based on inaccurate or insufficient data. This phenomenon is exacerbated by the ability of certain AI systems to 'learn' from data and make forecasts without any real supervision. If an AI system has been trained on a partial, incorrect or mislabelled database, it is likely to make erroneous predictions, thereby increasing the potential for malice or error. In such cases, the system can misidentify harmless elements as threats and react disproportionately.

Algorithmic biases also underline the importance of ongoing vigilance in the development of these technologies. It is essential that teams responsible for designing and deploying military AI provide rigorous supervision, have validation processes in place and are constantly alert to the possibility that their systems may reflect social, political or cultural biases. In addition, regular audits of algorithms, as well as tests on diverse populations and contexts, are crucial to ensuring that AI systems remain effective and fair. Collaboration with experts in ethics, human rights and sociology is essential to minimise the risk of discriminatory bias and improve the accountability of decisions made by AI systems in a military context.

In the absence of a binding international legal framework, each country is free to develop its own policies on autonomous weapons systems and military AI, resulting in uneven regulation at global level. Some countries, such as the United States and Israel, are investing massively in these technologies and deploying increasingly sophisticated systems, while others have neither the means nor the interest to invest in these innovations. This disparity in military capabilities and regulatory approaches has the potential to create new geopolitical imbalances, with the most technologically advanced nations enjoying a considerable strategic advantage over others. This raises important ethical questions about the proliferation of autonomous weapons systems and their potential to destabilise international relations.

In addition, the regulation of autonomous weapons raises significant practical challenges. The development of an international treaty to cover all aspects of the use of AI in warfare faces complex technical and diplomatic hurdles. For example, the question of how far automation can go without compromising human control over wartime decisions remains unanswered. Should we allow a high degree of autonomy for certain functions of weapons systems, or maintain total human control? If the answer is not clear-cut, it is because each country and each player has different interests depending on its strategic priorities and its vision of modern warfare.

Although efforts have been made to regulate the use autonomous technologies in times of conflict, the international legal framework remains largely inadequate to meet the challenges posed by the introduction of AI in the military sphere. The lack of specific regulations, the absence of consensus on the measures to be adopted, and the speed of technological advances make it difficult to draw up clear international standards. Until these challenges are overcome, the world will continue to navigate in an uncertain legal environment, where the risks of uncontrolled proliferation and abuse remain very real.

The acceleration in the development and integration of artificial intelligence in the military sphere raises a major challenge because of its direct impact on the global strategic balance. The lack of a solid regulatory framework and the desire of many countries to gain a technological advantage in this field are fuelling an arms race in which the speed of adoption of AI takes precedence over careful consideration of its consequences. The major military powers are investing considerable resources in these technologies, seeking to surpass their adversaries by developing increasingly autonomous and effective systems. This dynamic creates a climate of fierce competition in which each player, whether a State or a military coalition, is under constant pressure to innovate in order not to be outdone. However, this acceleration in the research and deployment of military AI outstripping regulation and control capabilities, opening the door to excessive and potentially uncontrollable militarisation of these technologies.

In such a context, AI becomes a factor that amplifies geopolitical tensions, as it alters the balance of power between nations. States with the most advanced technological resources are able to develop increasingly sophisticated autonomous weapons systems, giving them a considerable strategic advantage over those without such capabilities. This technological asymmetry increases the risks of instability, as it leads some countries to adopt circumvention strategies, in particular by investing in cyber espionage or seeking military alliances to compensate for their backwardness. It can also encourage states in a dominant position to adopt a more aggressive stance, in the knowledge that their technological superiority means they can intervene with less risk to their own forces. The emergence of AI in the military sphere is therefore not limited to a simple technological development: it is profoundly transforming the way in which conflicts are envisaged and managed, with potentially major repercussions for international stability.

Another major problem linked this technological arms race is the uncontrolled proliferation of autonomous weapons systems. As these technologies become more accessible, there is a risk that less scrupulous states, or even non-state actors such as terrorist groups or criminal organisations, will manage to appropriate them. Unlike nuclear weapons, the proliferation of which is tightly controlled by international treaties, AI systems applied to weapons do not require complex infrastructures or significant financial resources to develop. With the rapid advances in artificial intelligence, particularly in the area of open-source algorithms and computing capacity accessible via the cloud, it is becoming increasingly easy for unconventional players to equip themselves with advanced technologies. This phenomenon could lead to an increase in asymmetric conflicts, with non-state groups exploiting AI to carry out large-scale attacks with a minimum of human and material resources.

Another danger linked to the excessive militarisation of ΓIA is the gradual diminution of the human role in strategic decision-making. Although today ΓIA is mainly used to assist military commands by providing analyses and recommendations, its rapid evolution is leading to increasing dependence on these systems, to the point of entrusting them with critical tasks without human supervision. This raises major ethical issues, in particular the question of delegating the power to make lethal decisions to a machine. An AI, however advanced, has neither conscience nor moral judgement, which means that it can make decisions based solely on statistical models and optimisation calculations, without taking into account the human complexity of a war situation. If military decisions were to be taken by automated systems, the risk catastrophic errors or the uncontrolled escalation of conflicts would become a very real threat.

Finally, the acceleration of military ΓIA also raises the question of its impact on global strategic stability. As countries develop autonomous weapons systems, the fear of a military imbalance pushes other nations to invest massively in the same technologies, creating a vicious circle where each advance encourages technological one-upmanship. This phenomenon, often compared to the nuclear arms race of the 20th , can generate a widespread climate of mistrust between the major powers and encourage more aggressive deterrence strategies. In the absence of regulation, this dynamic can lead to a situation where states find themselves forced to use these technologies preventively, for fear that their adversaries will gain the upper hand first.

Artificial intelligence is now an essential part of the modern military landscape, providing armed forces with enhanced capabilities in terms of reconnaissance, logistics, cyber security and command. However, behind these technological advances lie major challenges and limitations that cannot be ignored. Despite its revolutionary potential, AI remains a technology that is dependent on data quality, prone to errors of judgement due to algorithmic biases, vulnerable to cyber attacks and difficult to regulate legally. Its integration into the military sphere raises profound ethical and strategic questions that require collective reflection and rigorous control mechanisms to avoid abuses and guarantee its use within a responsible framework.

One of the major concerns linked to the use of AI in the military field is the lack of a sufficiently robust international regulatory framework to govern its development and deployment. Unlike nuclear or biological weapons, which are the subject of strict treaties and international regulations, autonomous weapons systems do not yet benefit from a precise legislative framework. This lack of universal rules opens the door to divergent interpretations by different countries, each developing its own standards and strategies in line with its geopolitical and military interests. The regulatory efforts of bodies such as the United Nations are struggling to reach a consensus, because the major military powers, aware of the strategic advantages of AI, are reluctant to limit their own capabilities. This legal fragmentation increases the risk uncontrolled proliferation of military AI technologies, not only between states, but also between non-state actors likely to exploit these tools for malicious purposes.

Another fundamental challenge lies in the transparency and lack of explanation of the artificial intelligence systems used by the armed forces. Deep learning algorithms, although extremely powerful, often function like "black boxes", making it difficult to understand the precise mechanisms that lead to a decision. In a military context, this opacity poses serious problems, particularly when comes assigning responsibility in the event of an error. An AI that makes an erroneous decision by mistakenly targeting a civilian position or confusing an ally with an enemy raises fundamental questions about the chain of command and legal responsibility. Without transparency about AI decision-making processes, it becomes difficult to assess the compliance of military operations with the norms of international humanitarian law, making it potentially impossible to put in place effective control mechanisms to limit blunders and abuses.

So, while artificial intelligence offers undeniable opportunities to modernise and strengthen military capabilities, it cannot be seen as a miracle solution free of risks and limitations. AI will never replace human intelligence, or the moral and strategic considerations that must guide military decisions. It is imperative to put in place a clear regulatory framework, to strengthen the transparency and supervision of algorithms, to prevent algorithmic bias and to ensure that these technologies are developed and used in compliance with ethical and legal principles. A balance must be struck between technological innovation and human responsibility, so that artificial intelligence does not become an uncontrolled threat, but a tool in the service of security and international stability.

CHAPTER 3

Responsibility and control of autonomous systems

One of the first players likely to be implicated is **the designer of the AI system,** it a private company, a research laboratory or a military institution.

The role of the designer a military artificial intelligence system is fundamental in the chain of responsibility, as it is they who develop the algorithms, define the operating parameters and design the software architecture of these technologies. They may be private companies specialising in defence, university laboratories working in collaboration with governments, or military agencies developing their own systems in-house. The responsibility of the designers rests on several essential aspects: the quality of the algorithm, the robustness of the system, the management of potential biases and the implementation of rigorous security protocols to prevent errors and minimise risks. However, in a military context, where situations evolve rapidly and the decisions taken by the AI can have immediate and irreversible consequences, the responsibility of the designer is far from obvious.

One of the main challenges in designing military AI is system reliability. Software designed to make decisions in real time in a war environment must be designed to function optimally, whatever the external conditions. This means anticipating a wide range of scenarios, including unprecedented or unforeseen situations, prevent the AI from making an erroneous decision that could lead to human casualties or collateral damage. If an AI system has a technical flaw or programming error that causes it to misinterpret a situation - for example, by identifying an allied target as an enemy threat - the designer can be held liable, in the same way that a traditional arms manufacturer can be held liable if a weapon has a manufacturing defect. However, artificial intelligence, unlike a conventional weapon, does not perform a mechanical or pre-programmed action: it analyses, learns and makes decisions based on the data it processes, which complicates the attribution of liability.

The ability of military AI systems to adapt and learn further complicates the issue of responsibility. a guided missile that follows a precise, pre-programmed path, a military IA pent adjust its behaviour according to the information it receives and the situations it faces. This means that a designer may have developed a system that is apparently reliable and secure when it is put into service, but that this same system may evolve in an unpredictable way once deployed in the field. An IA that learns from its own decisions and modifies its way of acting may, in certain circumstances, adopt strategies not foreseen by its designers, or even develop undesirable behaviours due to unforeseen interactions with its environment. This poorly controlled learning complicates the identification of responsibility in the event of an error: if the AI makes a decision that was not foreseen or envisaged by its designers, can they still be considered responsible, or should the fault be attributed to the system itself?

Another crucial aspect of designers' responsibility lies in the cybersecurity of military AI systems. A poorly secured programme may be vulnerable to cyber attacks, which could allow an adversary to hack into or manipulate the AI for malicious purposes . Hijacked military AI can be used against the forces that deployed it, disable defence systems or even be reprogrammed to attack civilian targets. The responsibility of designers therefore extends to putting in place rigorous cyber security protocols and protection mechanisms against cyber attacks. However, the cyber threat is constantly evolving, and it is difficult to guarantee absolute protection against all forms of hacking. If a military AI system is hijacked by a hostile actor and causes unforeseen damage, can the designer be held responsible for failing to anticipate this flaw, or should the fault lie with the attacker who exploited the vulnerability?

Finally, the question of the responsibility of designers must be placed in a broader context, which includes the political and military players who decide to use these technologies in the field. An AI system, however sophisticated, remains a tool in the service of a military strategy defined by human authorities. Developers are not the only ones to play a role in the deployment and use of AI technologies: policymakers and military commanders also have a responsibility for how these systems are integrated into military operations. A military IA can be perfectly designed from a technical point of view, but misused in an operational context, leading to errors and disastrous consequences. Responsibility must therefore not be attributed solely to the developers, but must be shared between all the players involved in the decision-making chain.

Another level responsibility concerns **the user of the system.** The user of the artificial intelligence system, whether a soldier, an operator or a military commander, occupies a delicate position in the chain of responsibility linked to the use of military AI. Traditionally, armed forces are subject to the principles international humanitarian law, which imposes strict rules on the use of force, particularly with regard to the distinction between combatants and civilians, the proportionality of attacks and the need to avoid excessive collateral damage. When a human is control of a weapon or an intelligence system, he is directly responsible for the decisions taken, whether to engage in combat, launch an attack or assess a threat. However, the increasing integration of AI into military operations is changing this dynamic, as autonomous systems reduce or even eliminate human intervention in certain critical decisions. This raises a fundamental question: to what extent can the user be held responsible for an action carried out by a machine over which he has no direct control?

One of the main challenges of assigning responsibility to the user lies in the degree autonomy of military AI systems. If an IA functions as a decision support tool, providing recommendations or analyses that the human operator validates before acting, the user's responsibility is relatively clear. He retains an active role and remains in control of the decisions taken, which means that in the event of error or violation of international law, he can be held responsible for his choice to act on the basis of the information provided by the AI. However, when AI operates completely autonomously - for example, in the case of armed drones capable of identifying and engaging targets without human validation - the user loses much of his control over the decision-making process. In these cases, it becomes much more difficult to determine whether the military operator can be held responsible for an action that the AI has carried out without human intervention.

One of the most problematic scenarios is where a human operator activates a military AI system on the assumption that it will operate correctly, but the AI then makes an erroneous decision resulting in loss of life or violations of international law. Can the user then be held responsible for failing to monitor the AI adequately, even if it is supposed to be capable of operating autonomously? This type of situation poses a complex ethical and legal dilemma. In the current logic of the law of war, a combatant is held responsible for the acts he commits, but in the case of AI systems, the user may be completely overwhelmed by the unforeseen actions of the machine, which calls into question the possibility of imputing responsibility to the user.

Another key element to consider is the ability of users to

understand and anticipate how AI systems work. Machine learning and autonomous technologies are often referred to as "black boxes" because of the difficulty even their designers have in explaining precisely how they arrive at certain conclusions. This means that military operators can find themselves in a situation where they have to trust a system whose internal reasoning largely escapes them. If an IA makes a fatal error and the user did not have the technical means to foresee or prevent it, can he really be held responsible? Some experts believe that responsibility should be shared between the user and the system designers, but this approach poses other problems: how can this responsibility be shared fairly, and how much can a military user be expected to understand the mechanisms of a highly sophisticated AI in depth?

Furthermore, the increasing use of autonomous military AI is leading to a dilution of responsibility within the chains of command. In traditional military operations, orders are given by officers and executed by soldiers, which makes it possible clearly identify who is responsible in the event of error or failure. With AI, this traditional hierarchy is blurred, as part of the decision-making process is entrusted to a machine that can neither be judged nor be morally or legally responsible for its actions. This dilution of responsibility can encourage a certain disengagement on the part of users, who may be tempted to rely blindly on AI, assuming that it is acting optimally. This phenomenon, sometimes referred to as 'automation ', occurs when humans place excessive trust in technological systems and are reluctant to question their decisions, even when they evidence to suggest an error.

The issue of user responsibility is all the more delicate in contexts where AI systems are programmed to operate under time constraints, particularly in combat situations. In some military operations, it is necessary to act in a matter of seconds, which does not always give the user the opportunity to supervise or correct an action carried out by an IA. If an autonomous defence system shoots down a civil aircraft believing it has detected a threat, is the user liable when it had neither the time nor the means to intervene? Some legal experts are arguing for the establishment of "safeguards" that would guarantee significant human control over all critical decisions involving the use of lethal force, to prevent responsibility being transferred to a machine for which no one can really answer in court.

State responsibility for the use of military artificial intelligence systems is a major legal issue that raises many complex questions. Under international law, a State is held responsible for the acts of its armed forces, whether these acts are committed by soldiers, commanders or autonomous technologies put into service under its authority. This responsibility is based on the principles international humanitarian law, which requires states to comply with strict rules on the conduct of hostilities, the protection of civilians and proportionality in the use of force. Consequently, if a military AI system causes damage that violates these principles, the State that designed, deployed or used it can be held responsible before international judicial bodies such as the International Court of Justice (ICJ) or the International Criminal Court (ICC).

One of the main challenges associated with state responsibility lies in the difficulty of attributing a specific fante when the error is the product of a complex algorithm and autonomous operation. Unlike an action carried out directly by a soldier or officer, where responsibility can be determined on the basis of the orders given and the intentions displayed, a military IA can make decisions the basis of billions of variables, sometimes making it impossible to identify a precise wrongdoing. Can a state be held responsible if an IA acts unexpectedly, outside the scenarios envisaged when it was developed? To what extent can it be held culpable if the error results from a technical malfunction that even the experts had not anticipated? These questions illustrate the complexity applying the traditional rules of international law to autonomous systems whose operation is beyond any direct human intervention.

Another problem lies in the distinction between an intentional act and an accidental act. Under international law, a state can be held responsible it has knowingly used dangerous technology or failed to take the necessary precautions to avoid collateral damage. However, if a military IA operates unpredictably and causes human casualties due to a computer bug or faulty learning, can the State be considered to have committed an intentional fante? If the AI has been designed in accordance with current standards and subjected to rigorous testing before deployment, but nevertheless makes a serious error in the field, the State's responsibility may be challenged. This legal vagueness poses major difficulties for the implementation of sanctions or possible reparations in the event of violations of international law.

In addition, the question of state responsibility is closely linked to that of the chain of command and supervision. Military AI systems are often embedded in complex decision-making structures, where responsibilities are shared between several actors, including military commands, governments and the private companies that design these technologies. When an incident involving a IA occurs, it becomes difficult to determine whether the state is directly responsible or whether other parties must also be blamed. For example, if a reconnaissance IA mistakenly targets a humanitarian convoy and results in an unjustified air strike, does the blame lie with the state that used the technology, the company that developed it, or the engineers who designed the target recognition algorithm? This dilution of responsibility considerably complicates the implementation of legal sanctions and makes it more difficult to apply the principles of international justice.

Another major issue is that of the control and prevention mechanisms that States must put in place to regulate the use of IA militaries. International law requires States to take all necessary measures to avoid excessive damage and to ensure that their operations respect fundamental humanitarian principles. In the context of autonomous technologies, this means that states must invest in rigorous verification systems, thorough testing protocols and effective oversight procedures. However, in a technological race where speed deployment is often the priority, there is a risk that some states will fail to comply with these requirements and put insufficiently tested systems into service. This negligence could be considered as a breach of the law, making the State liable in the event of an incident.

The **legal vacuum surrounding ¡the use of artificial intelligence in the military sphere** is a major problem, not least because of the lack of a precise and binding international framework. While autonomous technologies are developing at an accelerating pace, the law of war is struggling to adapt to these new realities. The Geneva Conventions, adopted in the 20th century to regulate armed conflict and protect civilians, do not take into account the implications of autonomous and intelligent systems on the battlefield. They are based on the idea that responsibility is clearly attributable to human combatants, whether soldiers, commanders or states, but make no specific provision for weapons capable of taking independent decisions. This gap leaves uncertainty as to how the fundamental principles of international humanitarian law should be applied to AI systems, and how misconduct or violations committed by these technologies can be sanctioned.

Faced with this legal vagueness, several international

organisations, such as the United Nations, the International Committee of the Red Cross and various think tanks specialising in the law of war, are calling for an international treaty to regulate the use of military AI. The aim would be to ensure that these technologies respect the principles of distinction, proportionality and precaution that are at the heart of international humanitarian law. Such a treaty would impose strict rules on the use of autonomous weapons, limit their deployment in certain contexts and establish control mechanisms to ensure that they are not misused. Some experts believe that a clear regulatory framework would not only reduce the risk of accidents and abuse, but would also encourage more responsible use of AI in military operations, by preventing scenarios where these systems are used without proper supervision.

The speed with which AI technologies are evolving makes it even more difficult to put in place appropriate legislation. The development cycles of autonomous systems are much faster than those of international legislative processes, which means that any attempt at regulation is likely to be quickly overtaken by new technological advances. Even if a treaty were be adopted today, it may no longer be relevant in a few years' time because of the emergence of new generations of AI systems with even more sophisticated capabilities. This dynamic poses a major challenge for regulators, who must strike a balance between the need to impose strict standards and the flexibility required to adapt to technological developments.

Another point of tension lies in the issue of transparency and verification. Even if an international agreement were to be reached to regulate military AI, how can we be sure that states will actually honour their commitments? Unlike nuclear weapons, which require heavy and detectable infrastructures, the development of military AI relies on software that can be modified, distributed and updated discreetly. It would therefore be difficult for an international organisation to monitor effectively whether a country is complying with the limitations imposed by a treaty, or whether it is secretly pursuing research into unauthorised autonomous weapons systems. This difficulty in monitoring and enforcement is a major obstacle to the adoption of an effective regulatory framework.

The legal vacuum surrounding the use of military artificial intelligence is therefore a central issue that requires an urgent and concerted response from the international community. As long as the major powers fail to reach agreement on the rules to be established, the risks associated with the development and use of these technologies will continue to grow, with potentially serious implications for global security. Increased cooperation between states, international organisations and experts in the law of war is essential to avoid uncontrolled drift and to ensure that military AI is used responsibly, in accordance with the fundamental principles of international humanitarian law.

The adoption of a principle of shared responsibility appears to be a potentially viable solution for regulating the use of artificial intelligence systems in the military field and ensuring that no actor can escape its obligations in the event of an incident. One of the main issues associated with autonomous technologies is the difficulty of assigning responsibility to a seni responsible when these systems make decisions independently. By distributing responsibility between several levels - designers, users and States - it would be possible to ensure better control of military AI systems while avoiding situations where no party can be held responsible on the grounds that the AI has acted unpredictably.

However, responsibility cannot be laid solely at the door of the designers. The users of AI systems, i.e. the soldiers and operators who deploy them in the field, also have a role to play . A clear legal framework needs to be put in place to govern the training of soldiers and officers in the use of autonomous technologies, emphasising the importance of appropriate human supervision. In cases where l'IA would operate in semi-autonomous mode, the operator would be responsible for validating or overturning its decisions, which would imply a duty of vigilance and an obligation to follow strict protocols. If an error occurs due to misuse or lack of supervision, the operator could be held responsible, in the same way as a pilot who fails to follow safety procedures when operating a fighter jet.

Another fundamental aspect of this model of shared responsibility lies in putting in place mechanisms assess the extent to which an error is attributable to a design fault, misuse by the operator or a political decision by the military command. It would be necessary to create specific investigation to analyse incidents involving autonomous systems, combining expertise of artificial intelligence specialists, lawyers and military personnel. Such an approach would provide a better understanding of the origin of errors and prevent any single party from being unfairly held responsible. These investigations can be carried out by national authorities, but also by independent international bodies to guarantee a certain impartiality and prevent states from trying to minimise their involvement in controversial incidents.

The integration of a responsible and ethical IA in the military field is based on the introduction of legislative and technical safeguards to ensure that these technologies are used in a controlled manner and in accordance with the principles international law. A principle of shared responsibility would be a major step forward in this direction, preventing errors or abuses from going unpunished and encouraging all the players involved to act with caution. However, implementing such a model will require considerable efforts in terms of regulation, international cooperation and transparency. Only a concerted approach will prevent military AI from becoming a lawless zone, where the damage caused cannot be attributed to any identifiable responsible party.

The question of **the responsibility of** ¡military **artificial intelligence** goes far beyond the legal framework and raises fundamental ethical issues that call into question the place of technology in warfare. One of the most sensitive debates concerns the possibility of entrusting a machine with the power to decide on life and death. This issue calls into question the very nature of military engagement, in which human decision-making has always played a central role, particularly in terms of discernment, morality and adaptation to the complex and unforeseen situations of the battlefield.

In the face of these risks, many experts and humanitarian organisations are calling for a total ban on the use of autonomous light weapons. They believe that it is morally unacceptable to delegate life-and-death decisions to machines, because no artificial intelligence can guarantee absolute respect for human values and the principles humanitarian law. The International Committee of the Red Cross, along with a number of non-governmental organisations, is campaigning for the adoption of an international treaty banning the use of fully autonomous weapons, along the same lines as the ban on chemical weapons and anti-personnel mines. In their view, the lack of clear responsibility for the use of these technologies and the risk fatal errors justify strict and immediate regulation.

Other specialists, on the other hand, believe that military AI technologies can be framed by strict rules and human supervision mechanisms that would guarantee their ethical and controlled use. Rather than banning these systems, they advocate an approach based on "supervised autonomy", where AI can be used to assist the armed forces in decision-making, without ever being left alone to determine the outcome of an attack. One of the fundamental principles of this approach is the maintenance of a "human loop", i.e. a system in which human intervention remains necessary to validate critical actions, in particular the use of lethal force. This model seeks to avoid the scenario of an AI operating without human control and making irreparable errors. However, even in a framework where human supervision is maintained, the attribution of responsibility remains a thorny issue. If a military operator validates a decision based on an erroneous FIA analysis, who should be held responsible? The AI itself cannot be judged, and the operator can invoke the trust placed in the algorithms to absolve himself of all responsibility.

Finally, the question of the responsibility of military FIA also extends to the long-term consequences of these technologies on global security. Uncontrolled proliferation of autonomous weapons could lead to increased risks instability, particularly if these technologies fall into the hands non-state groups or malicious actors. Unlike traditional weapons, which require specific military training and infrastructure, AI systems can be used by terrorist groups or rogue states without the need for advanced military expertise. This poses the risk a democratisation of automated warfare, where attacks can be carried out without direct human intervention, making deterrence and conflict prevention more difficult.

The question of legal liability in the event of damage caused by military artificial intelligence represents a major issue in the framing of these technologies, which is still largely unexplained and constantly evolving. As AI plays an increasingly important role in military strategies, complex challenges arise concerning the attribution of liability in the event of accidents, violations of international humanitarian law, unforeseen consequences resulting from the use of autonomous systems. The lack of a specific legal framework to govern these situations, combined with the autonomous nature of algorithms, makes it difficult to establish clear and effective liability mechanisms.

This uncertainty about responsibility has far-reaching consequences, not only for the victims of errors committed by ΠA, but also for the military actors themselves, who may find themselves in a situation where their own use of an uncontrollable technology escapes any form of control or foresight. Furthermore, the absence of a clear legal framework on this issue also poses a significant risk to the application of international humanitarian law. The law of war, as codified in the Geneva Conventions and other international instruments, is based on fundamental principles, notably the distinction between combatants and civilians, and the principle of proportionality of attacks. However, these principles can be compromised when decisions are taken by machines that cannot exercise moral discernment or human judgement. In situations where autonomous systems are deployed to target enemies, the lack of direct human control can lead to mistaken attacks, strikes on civilians or breaches of the rules of combat. If such an incident occurs, the question of responsibility becomes particularly complex, as it becomes difficult to know who should be held responsible: the creator of the system, the state that deployed it , or the military operator,

often caught in a high-pressure environment where its choices can be limited by ΓIA's capabilities.

The lack of regulation and clear responsibilities for the use of autonomous technologies in war could also lead to abuses, with AI becoming an uncontrollable tool of war. In the absence of supervision and a rigorous legal framework, it is difficult to imagine how these technologies can be used responsibly. Such a development could lead to excessive militarisation of AI,

increasing the risk of conflict and violence, while reducing human responsibility in warfare. In scenarios where machines decide on the use of lethal force without human intervention, the fundamental principles of justice, fairness and respect for human rights would be compromised.
It is therefore becoming imperative for the international community to make a decisive commitment to establishing clear legal rules concerning the liability of military AI systems. The development of an appropriate international framework must meet several objectives: clarifying responsibilities in the event of damage caused by autonomous IA, ensuring that these technologies comply with international humanitarian law, and guaranteeing that decision-making remains rooted in ethical and humane principles. To achieve this, it is necessary to strengthen international cooperation processes in order to draw up clear and binding rules capable of guaranteeing the controlled and responsible use of military technologies. Efforts must focus on setting up control mechanisms to assess the risks associated with ΓIA before they are deployed, and on establishing accountability mechanisms to avoid impunity in the event of failure or violation of international standards.
AI offers undeniable potential for improving the accuracy, efficiency and speed of military operations, but it must not be deployed lightly. With the advent of advanced technologies, it becomes crucial to ensure that the use of AI in the military domain is subject to strict accountability and appropriate oversight, prevent artificial intelligence from becoming an uncontrollable tool of war, with no legal or ethical safeguards.

CHAPTER 4

Towards regulation of autonomous autonomous weapons

The growing use of autonomous lethal weapon systems (ALWS) is raising major concerns in the international community. These systems, which have greater autonomy in decision-making, raise major military, legal, ethical and humanitarian issues. While these technologies offer exceptional technical capabilities, enabling greater precision and a potential reduction in human casualties on the ground, they also come with serious risks for global security and the stability of armed conflicts. The introduction of SALA into the military arsenals of states is, in effect, transforming the very nature of modern warfare, by sidelining human responsibility in decisions that have dramatic consequences, particularly as regards violations of international humanitarian law and the moral principles underlying warfare.

One of the most hotly debated issues at international level is whether these weapons should be regulated or even banned. There are many voices in favour of an international treaty ban or significantly restrict the use of SALW. The idea of a prohibition treaty is supported by those who believe that delegating the decision of life and death to machines, without adequate human supervision, represents a fundamental break with the principles humanitarian law. Those in favour of banning SALA argue that, because of their autonomy, these can lead to erroneous, unpredictable and potentially catastrophic decisions, particularly if the machines are unable to take into account the human and moral context in which they operate. From this perspective, SALAs would be seen as a threat both to international security, by encouraging a new arms race, and to humanity, by eliminating the possibility of moral judgement in war situations.

However, other countries and players, often the major military powers, take a more nuanced view. Rather than rejecting the idea of SALAs altogether, they argue in favour of their strict regulation. From this perspective, SALAs can continue to exist, but under strict conditions governing their development and use. These players believe that SALAs can have considerable benefits in terms of reducing soldier casualties and improving the effectiveness of military operations, while minimising human error. They argue that, to control the risks, a comprehensive regulatory framework can be put in place to ensure that these systems respect fundamental principles such as the distinction between combatants and civilians, proportionality in attacks and the need for human oversight in critical decision-making processes. In this way,

The introduction of SALA into modern armies would not be a threat to the principles humanitarian law, but rather a controlled and ethically supervised technological advance.

The debate on the regulation of SALA is also a debate on the very nature of human control in wartime. On the one hand, there are those who believe that no machine can ever replace the moral discernment of a human in the specific context of each military situation. On the other hand, there are those who see in these technologies an opportunity to limit human error and improve the precision of military interventions, which could, in theory, reduce overall human suffering. This opens the way to a variety of proposals aimed at regulating SALAs rather than banning them outright.

The lack of consensus is largely due to fundamental differences between the military powers. For example, some countries, such as the United States, Russia and China, have emphasised their desire to retain a certain freedom of technological innovation and to develop autonomous systems as part of their national defence strategies, without too many international constraints. These countries consider that the regulation of SALA is linked to their military capabilities and their strategic position on the world stage. Conversely, other nations, notably those in the European Union, are much more inclined to strictly regulate these technologies, arguing that effective regulation is necessary to avoid abuses in the field and to guarantee respect for international humanitarian law. This geopolitical divide, linked to differences in military strategies and national priorities, complicates the development of a global legal framework that can be adopted by all.

In parallel to the discussions under the aegis of the United Nations, several other initiatives have emerged to encourage the regulation of SALA. Some non-governmental organisations (NGOs), such as Human Rights Watch and the International Committee of the Red Cross (ICRC), have been actively advocating an international treaty banning autonomous lethal weapons. They stress that the use of these technologies can lead to violations of human rights and the principles of international humanitarian law, particularly because of the impossibility of carrying out real-time human monitoring in the field. At the same time, initiatives have been launched by groups of countries, such as the Campaign to Ban Autonomous Lethal Weapons, to make States aware of the need to act quickly before uncontrolled proliferation of these systems has dramatic consequences.

Ultimately, the question of whether SALAs should be banned altogether or simply regulated remains a central issue in international discussions. This debate is all the more crucial as it raises profound questions about the nature of modern warfare and the extent of human control we wish to maintain over the machines that take part in acts of war. For the time being, it seems that the most promising approach would be to find a compromise that combines strict regulation with respect for the fundamental principles of warfare, while taking account of the inevitable technological advances in this field. The role of the United Nations and international cooperation will be decisive in establishing a global legal framework to prevent abuses and guarantee the ethical and responsible use of SALA in armed conflicts.

One of the major responses to the rise of Autonomous Lethal Weapon Systems (ALWS) has been to advocate the establishment of an international treaty that would specifically ban these weapons. This initiative is in line with existing treaties, such as those banning chemical or biological weapons, and seeks to respond to the growing fear that these technologies will become uncontrollable instruments of war. Proponents of this approach stress that it is imperative to take preventive action to limit the development of SALA and prevent them from becoming an integral part of the world's military arsenals. In this context, a prohibition treaty would be seen as an effective means of preventing a technological escalation that could redefine not only armed conflict, but also the way in which war-related decisions are taken, with potentially devastating consequences.

Arguments in favour a prohibition treaty also point out that the introduction of SALA could lead to violations of international humanitarian law (IHL), particularly with regard to the distinction between combatants and civilians, and respect for the principle of proportionality in attacks. Indeed, one of the fundamental principles of IHL is that attacks must be carried out in such a way as to protect civilians and avoid human casualties disproportionate to the military objective sought. In this context, the ability of machines to distinguish between legitimate military targets and innocent civilian populations becomes a fundamental issue. AI systems, despite their advances, remain fallible, and there are concerns that even sophisticated AI may not properly grasp the nuances of the war terrain, particularly in situations where civilians are intricately intertwined with military actors. For example, an autonomous system could make erroneous decisions based on incomplete or biased data, or on simplified interpretations of a complex situation, leading to unjustified attacks on innocent people.

At the heart of this issue is the fundamental notion of responsibility. In past wars, responsibility for military decisions, including those involving the loss of human life, rested with the leaders and operators of weapons systems. But with SALA, this responsibility can be diluted, posing a major legal and ethical challenge. By entrusting a machine with the power to decide the fate of human lives, we introduce the possibility of a disconnection between military actions and the responsibilities of human decision-makers. Machines, although extremely powerful and capable of calculating probabilities, lack the capacity for moral judgement. This lack of human discernment makes the idea of a machine, rather than a human being, deciding on life and death on the battlefield legitimately alarming.

The idea of entrusting such a capability to a IA is seen by some experts as a fundamental break with the human and moral values that underpin the laws of war. War, although a scourge, remains a complex reality where human, ethical and legal considerations must take precedence. In this sense, supporters of treaty banning SALA assert that decisions on the use of lethal force, particularly in such serious situations, must always involve some form of human control, ensuring that decisions are taken not only on the basis of military effectiveness, but also according to principles of justice and humanity.

Defenders of the ban on autonomous lethal weapon systems (ALWS) point to a number of fundamental concerns linked to the very nature of these weapons and their implications for modern warfare. One of the most frequent criticisms concerns the ability of ALWS to operate autonomously, i.e. without any direct human intervention in the decision-making process. This decision-making autonomy, while technically impressive, raises major ethical and legal questions. Indeed, those in favour of banning AAS believe that the possibility of machines taking lethal decisions on human lives - particularly in the context war - is deeply problematic. Machines, in the absence of moral discernment, do not have the capacity to judge situations according to ethical criteria, which makes them incapable of taking decisions that respect the fundamental principles of international humanitarian law (IHL), in particular the distinction between combatants and civilians, and the proportionality of attacks.

A central aspect of the argument of those opposed to the use of SALAs is the fear that these systems could be responsible for unjustified strikes or erroneous attacks against non-military targets, or against civilians. SALAs, because of their programming and data-driven learning, can misinterpret complex situations and lead to actions that do not conform to international norms. For example, in chaotic war environments where the distinction between combatants and civilians is blurred, an IA may, based on the information available to it, incorrectly identify civilians as legitimate targets, resulting in massive and unnecessary loss of life. Furthermore, autonomous systems, depending on their algorithms, can make decisions based solely on military criteria, without taking into account the humanitarian impact, which considerably increases the risk of human rights violations. The failure to take account of moral assessment and the long-term consequences of strikes is seen as a major flaw in these systems.

The answer to these concerns, according to these advocates, lies in the creation of a binding international treaty that would definitively prohibit the deployment of SALA. Such a treaty would be based on the principle that no weapons system should be allowed to make lethal decisions without human oversight, and that it is imperative that any military action that respects human rights and the laws of war remain under direct human control. This treaty can draw on historical precedents for the regulation of weapons of mass destruction, such as chemical, biological and nuclear weapons, the production, possession and use of which have been strictly limited at international level. For those in favour of banning SALW, a global legal framework prohibiting these autonomous weapons would ensure that humanity does not lose control over its own decisions in warfare and would thus protect the fundamental principles of international humanitarian law, in particular the protection of civilians and the preservation of human dignity in wartime.

Advocates of treaty banning SALA stress that preventive action is essential to prevent these systems from being deployed on a large scale without a sufficient legal framework. In their view, it is imperative to ensure that military decision-making remains under human responsibility, in order to avoid the dehumanisation of combat, prevent massive human rights violations and preserve the integrity of international humanitarian law in an increasingly technological world.

However, a camp opposed to a total ban on autonomous lethal weapon systems (ALWS) is putting forward arguments based on the strategic and operational advantages that these technologies can offer, both from a military and humanitarian point of view. This group, made up mainly of military powers and industry players, argues that SALAs have the potential to revolutionise the way conflicts are fought by enabling more precise and targeted strikes, while reducing the risks to soldiers and minimising the errors of judgement often associated with human intervention in the field.

One of the main arguments put forward by those in favour of the use of AAS is their ability to carry out highly accurate strikes. In theory, autonomous systems can rapidly analyse massive quantities of data and assess the situation more objectively than human beings, eliminating a large proportion of human errors caused by fatigue, stress or emotion. For example, an autonomous drone equipped with sophisticated AI can identify and neutralise specific military targets while reducing the likelihood of hitting civilians or committing collateral damage. The ability of these weapons to operate with great precision could, according to the supporters of this technology, enable more surgical strikes and, consequently, save human lives by limiting unnecessary destruction.

Beyond the immediate military benefits, some SALA advocates also believe that these technologies can be used to minimise errors of judgement in war situations. Artificial intelligence, they argue, can make decisions based on strictly defined parameters and without human bias, which would avoid certain types of classic error, such as excessive or disproportionate retaliatory attacks. AI can be programmed to scrupulously respect the principles of international humanitarian law, making decisions based solely on objective criteria such as the legitimacy of targets, the proportionality attacks and the minimisation collateral damage. From this point of view, the argument is that the machine, although lacking in moral sense, can carry missions more accurately and fairly than humans because of the elimination of certain emotional or subjective factors that sometimes influence human decisions in the field.

In view of these advantages, SALA proponents reject the idea a total ban, arguing that the risks and ethical abuses can be kept in check by strict and controlled regulation. They therefore propose an international legal framework that would establish clear rules for the design, use and control of autonomous weapons systems, while ensuring that these weapons respect the fundamental principles of international humanitarian law and human rights. They believe that, rather than banning these technologies, it is more appropriate to establish rigorous protocols and control mechanisms to ensure that they are used only in specific situations, defined by criteria of proportionality, necessity and discrimination.

Advocates of regulation rather than prohibition also see regulation as a means of promoting a healthy technological competition, in which different countries and companies can work together to guarantee high standards of safety, respect for human rights and control. Rather than innovation, they believe that regulation would channel development efforts to ensure that these technologies are used responsibly and in accordance with humanitarian principles. Such a framework should encourage international collaboration, particularly within the United Nations, to develop universal safety standards that limit the risks of escalation and encourage a collective approach to the management of these weapons.

The proposals for the regulation of Autonomous Lethal Weapon Systems (ALWS) aim to introduce control mechanisms and strict limits to govern their development and use in the field. These proposals focus a number of fundamental aspects, including the transparency of algorithms, human supervision, the definition of appropriate contexts of use, and liability in the event of failure of these technologies.

One of the most important proposals is to establish transparency criteria for the algorithms that drive these systems. The argument behind this proposal is that, in order to guarantee the ethical and legally compliant use of SALAs, it is imperative that the decision-making processes of the IA be understandable, verifiable and accessible to all the actors involved, including the judicial authorities and external observers. The complexity of the algorithms underlying these technologies must be such that the decisions taken by SALAs can be clearly traced and explained. This means that the principles and logic used by these systems to identify targets, assess the proportionality of attacks or distinguish between combatants and civilians must be publicly available and audited. This transparency would not only strengthen the confidence of the parties involved, but also prevent the abuses associated with excessive automation of military decisions, particularly in contexts where errors can have catastrophic consequences.

Another central proposition in the regulation of SALA is the need maintain human supervision, even if the artificial intelligence takes autonomous decisions in the field. Many regulations insist on the importance of maintaining a "human control" in the key stages of the decision-making process, particularly in the targeting and attack phase. The principle of human supervision ensures that, even when autonomous systems carry out an analysis and propose actions, a human operator must be able to intervene to validate or rectify these decisions, especially in situations where ethical, legal or humanitarian considerations are at stake. This is part of a framework in which humans retain ultimate responsibility for the decision, ensuring a balance between technological efficiency and compliance with international humanitarian law standards.

In addition to human supervision, some proposals envisage the establishment of "non-autonomy zones", in which the use of AAS would be strictly prohibited. This concept is based on the idea that there are contexts where decision-making absolutely must remain in the hands of a human being, in order to guarantee respect for the fundamental principles of international humanitarian law. For example, in areas where civilians are in close proximity or where it difficult to make a clear distinction between combatants and non-combatants, it would be unacceptable to let a machine alone decide the fate of individuals. These non-autonomy zones can also be set up in environments where the situation evolves rapidly and where human judgement remains essential to take account of moral, ethical and contextual factors. The aim of such restrictions would be to preserve the primacy of the human in critical decisions and to protect the rights of civilians in contexts where the dehumanisation of military decisions would be a direct consequence of the automation of warfare processes.

Another crucial aspect of the regulation of SALA concerns the question of liability in the event of failure or error. The autonomous nature of these weapons raises complex questions about the apportionment of responsibility in the event of violations of the laws war, particularly if these weapons commit illegal acts, such as attacks on civilians or unjustified destruction. The proposed regulations also include the establishment of mechanisms for verifying, monitoring and tracing SALA actions. This means that every decision taken by an autonomous weapon, from identifying the target to the strike itself, should be recorded and traceable, in order to determine who is responsible in the event of an incident. These mechanisms aim to ensure that, even if a machine takes the decision to attack, it is always possible to trace the source of the incident and to hold those responsible - whether designers, operators or military leaders - to account for their actions. The traceability of SALA actions would be essential not only to identify those responsible, but also to provide a basis of proof in the event of judicial investigations and to guarantee that responsibility remains human and not solely attributed to a machine.

The regulation proposals also emphasise the need to define

precise criteria for the use of these systems. These criteria would include restrictions on the types of missions for which SALAs can be deployed. For example, SALAs should only be used in contexts where military action is strictly necessary and where the use of an autonomous weapon does not violate the principles of war, notably proportionality and discrimination. The use criteria should also specify the extent to which human operators must be trained and prepared to supervise SALAs, to ensure that they understand the capabilities and limitations of autonomous systems.

Finally, for these regulations to be effective, they should be accompanied a framework for international cooperation. The development, use and regulation of SALAs cannot be limited to national or regional initiatives alone, as their impact transcends borders. The international community, through institutions such as the United Nations, must play a central role in the development and implementation of binding international norms that ensure the safety and legality of autonomous weapon systems. This involves creating international monitoring mechanisms, promoting transparency, and encouraging the development of codes of conduct and best practice on a global scale. The idea is to create a unified legal framework that can reduce the risk of uncontrolled proliferation of AAS and ensure that these technologies are used responsibly and in compliance with international standards.

Since 2014, discussions on SALAs have become increasingly important within the CCW, with the establishment of a Group Governmental Experts (GGE) tasked examining the implications of these systems and proposing regulatory measures. The main task of the GGE, made up of representatives of the Member States, was to analyse the risks and challenges associated with SALA, particularly with regard to their compliance with international humanitarian law. The GGE organised several discussion sessions during which experts presented the legal, ethical and technical issues relating to the use of these weapons. Among the major issues addressed were questions of responsibility, the distinction between combatants and civilians, and proportionality in strikes.

The discussions also highlighted the need a clear normative framework to regulate the use of SALA, and many experts suggested the idea a total or partial ban on these weapons. However, despite these concerns, no consensus has yet been reached on exactly how to regulate these weapons. The debates have revealed deep-seated differences between Member States, particularly between the major military powers, which have different strategic visions of the future of warfare and the role of technology in conflict.

The United States, Russia and China, for example, have been particularly reticent about adopting restrictions on SALAs, as they believe that such limitations may harm their competitiveness and their ability to maintain a strategic advantage in defence. These countries invest massively in the development of advanced military technologies, including autonomous weapons systems, and fear that a ban treaty or overly strict regulations could compromise their ability to conduct military operations in an effective and modern manner. They see the research and development of advanced military technologies, such as SALA, as essential to guaranteeing their sovereignty and national security in the face of growing threats. These differences have hampered the development of a coherent international legal framework, despite calls from many other countries and non-governmental organisations for stricter regulation.

To date, although constructive discussions have taken place, the CCW has been unable to reach a global agreement on the need for a treaty banning LAS. Instead, some states are proposing strict regulation that would set clear limits on the use of these technologies, while allowing nations to continue to develop and deploy autonomous systems under controlled and supervised conditions. This approach of regulation rather than outright prohibition reflects the position of several major military powers which, while recognising the potential dangers of AAS, wish to avoid any limitations that could hamper their technological innovation and competitiveness in the defence field.

The deadlock between the major powers on the SALA issue illustrates the challenges of international diplomacy in the field of security, where national strategic interests can take precedence over humanitarian concerns and the objectives of international regulation. In a context where the militarisation of new technologies is perceived as a key factor in global power and influence, it is difficult to reach a compromise between the nations that develop these technologies and those that advocate more rigorous control mechanisms.

However, the United Nations has continued to play an important role in encouraging collective reflection on the future of SALA, coordinating discussions between Member States and gathering contributions from civil society, experts and international organisations, such as the International Committee of the Red Cross, which have stressed the importance of maintaining principles accountability and respect for international humanitarian law. The United Nations has also encouraged the adoption of non-binding resolutions and declarations, which although they do not have direct legal effect, serve to raise international awareness of the risks associated with SALA.

The United Nations' position is based on a fundamental principle: war must continue to be governed by rules that protect civilians and limit human suffering. The introduction of autonomous weapons systems that can potentially act without human intervention raises questions about the ability to guarantee these principles. If an autonomous system causes disproportionate damage or strikes civilian targets, the question arises as to who should be held responsible. This legal vacuum is one of the most pressing issues to be addressed in these discussions.

The role of the United Nations in the SALA debate has become increasingly central, not only in initiating discussions and promoting regulatory solutions, but also in mobilising a global dialogue between States, experts and civil society. The ultimate goal is to establish an international framework that reconciles national security imperatives with ethical and humanitarian concerns. Ultimately, while the process of regulating SALA is still under way, it is clear that the United Nations will have to play an essential mediating role to ensure that the deployment of these technologies does not take place at the expense of fundamental human values and respect for international standards of humanitarian law.

The United Nations is at the heart of international discussions concerning the regulation of autonomous lethal weapon systems (SALA). Since 2014, the UN Conventional Arms Forum (CCW) has intensified discussions on this topic, establishing a Group Governmental Experts (GGE) dedicated to examining the implications of SALAs and discussing their regulation. However, despite these efforts, no global consensus has been reached adopting a ban treaty or introducing strict regulations. Differences between major military powers, such as the United States, Russia and China, have hampered the development of a common international legal framework.

In November 2022, Human Rights Watch and the Harvard International Human Rights Law Clinic published a report entitled "An Agenda for Action: Alternative Processes for Negotiating a Killer Robots Treaty", suggesting the creation of a new international forum to negotiate a treaty on autonomous weapons. The report was presented at a conference in Geneva, reflecting growing concerns about the lack of effective regulation of SALAs.

It is regrettable that at the 7(e) edition of the Paris Peace Forum, held on 11 and 12 November 2024, the discussions focused mainly on the need for effective international governance in the face of today's global challenges, and that the role of artificial intelligence in armed conflicts was only touched on in passing. The central theme was "In search of a world order works". On the fringes of this forum, a specific meeting[4] was organised to discuss the evolution of artificial intelligence (AI) in the military context. This session highlighted the risks associated with the use of AI in armed conflicts, particularly with regard to combat drones and automated targeting systems. The experts expressed concern about the dehumanisation of military decisions and the potential for uncontrolled escalation of conflicts.

The debate on the regulation of Autonomous Lethal Weapon Systems (ALWS) is complex and marked by a series of diplomatic, political and strategic obstacles. One of the main challenges is the slow pace of diplomatic processes and the difficulty of reaching consensus among nations. The development of binding international rules requires consensus, which is often difficult to achieve because of the diversity of national interests and divergent strategic priorities. Each country approaches the SALA issue according to its own security needs, technological capabilities and geopolitical ambitions. This makes the creation of a coherent and unified international legal framework particularly complex.

The discrepancy between ethical and humanitarian concerns on

4 Le Monde, 11 November 2024 "The evolution of artificial intelligence in warfare risks marking a new dark era for our species".

the one hand, and national security imperatives on the other, represents one of the greatest obstacles to the regulation of SALA. While some believe that it is necessary to regulate these technologies in order to preserve the principles of international law and protect civilian populations, others see regulation as a threat to their national security and military competitiveness. This divide makes diplomatic negotiations on the issue particularly difficult, as there is no consensus on how to reconcile the protection of human rights and the security needs of states.

The slow pace of negotiations and diplomatic processes, coupled with divergent strategic interests, make it extremely difficult to develop a unified international response to the threat posed by SALA. The lack of a common political will and the influence of the major military powers are slowing down adoption of binding measures. Dialogue between nations, although essential for establishing standards, is coming up against resistance that makes the achievement of concrete solutions uncertain. This slowness in putting in place appropriate regulations accentuates the need to define clear international rules quickly, before the risks associated with SALA become unmanageable and further destabilise global security.

In this complex context, where the divergence of interests between States and diplomatic obstacles make it difficult to adopt a global and binding regulation of autonomous lethal weapon systems (ALWS), it is likely that the long-term solution lies in a gradual approach. This approach would make it possible to reach progressive agreements on specific aspects of the use of these technologies before arriving a complete and global framework. Rather than imposing a uniform global treaty from the outset, a series of targeted initiatives at different levels may allow the regulation of SALA to progress in a more pragmatic and less confrontational way.

Such an approach could include regional agreements. Such agreements would be particularly effective in geopolitical areas where there are common concerns about the proliferation of autonomous military technologies. For example, in regions where military tensions are particularly high, such as East Asia, the Middle East or Eastern Europe, countries may decide to enter into bilateral or multilateral discussions on how to limit or control the deployment of SALA. These discussions may focus on specific aspects, such as limiting the use of these systems in sensitive areas or establishing transparency measures on their development and deployment. Such an approach would make it possible to create regional standards adapted to local geopolitical realities, while limiting the proliferation of these technologies in high-risk areas.

The commitment of international organisations such as the International Committee of the Red Cross (ICRC) also plays a crucial role in this dynamic. As an independent humanitarian institution, the ICRC is deeply involved in promoting respect for international humanitarian law and ethical standards in times conflict. It has particular legitimacy to raise awareness of the issue of SALW and to promote standards of conduct that take account of the fundamental principles of warfare, such as the distinction between civilians and combatants, the need to minimise human suffering and to ensure proportionality in attacks. The ICRC's role is multifaceted: as well as lobbying for international agreements, the organisation can also mediate and facilitate discussions between states. Through its reports, studies and appeals for action, the ICRC can raise public awareness worldwide and encourage governments to take concrete measures to prevent an uncontrolled arms race.

As part of this incremental approach, it is also important to consider monitoring and verification mechanisms to ensure that the incremental agreements adopted at each stage are effectively respected. These mechanisms may include independent monitoring of SALA deployments, regular audits of the systems and public reporting on their use. In addition, sanctions or retaliatory measures can be envisaged for States that fail to comply with the agreements reached, thereby reinforcing the effectiveness of these initiatives.

This gradual approach would make it possible to take account of the rapid pace of technological development and the diversity of national needs and concerns. Until a comprehensive, global framework is adopted, significant progress can be made through gradual compromises and sectoral agreements. This method would also have the advantage of allowing greater flexibility, leaving room for adjustments in line with new technological discoveries or changes in the geopolitical landscape. It would also encourage greater cooperation between states and international organisations, such as the ICRC, which could play a pivotal role in developing the ethical and legal standards that would guide the future of SALW.

Although significant progress has been made in discussions on the regulation of Autonomous Lethal Weapon Systems (ALWS), it is clear that many challenges remain before a comprehensive, clear and binding legal framework can be put in place. Indeed, the SALA issue is not just about technological advances themselves, but also about the impact they have on international security, the stability of relations between States, and above all on respect for the fundamental norms of international law, particularly in terms of humanitarian law and human rights. The international community therefore faces a complex task: carefully weighing up the benefits and risks associated with these increasingly sophisticated warfare technologies, while striving to strike a delicate balance between innovation, security and ethical values.

One of the first challenges is the uncertainty and rapidity with which these technologies evolve. Because of their decision-making autonomy, SALAs bring new capabilities to the battlefield. In theory, they can reduce human casualties by reducing direct human intervention and increasing the precision of strikes. However, this very autonomy raises major concerns, not least the lack of moral discernment of these machines. An IA has neither a moral conscience nor the ability to judge the human consequences of its actions within an ethical framework. The automation of life and death decisions on the battlefield introduces a break with the fundamental principles of the law of war, such as the need to differentiate between civilians and combatants and to respect the proportionality of attacks. It is this tension between the promises technological innovation and the ethical challenges that constitutes one of the main obstacles to the regulation of SALA.

Discussions to date have shown that, although there is a desire to regulate these weapons, opinions remain deeply divided, particularly among the major military powers. On the one hand, some states, particularly those investing heavily in defence technologies, fear that overly stringent regulations could hamper their ability to maintain a strategic advantage. The idea a total ban on SALA seems difficult to accept for these nations, who feel that such a measure could unbalance their competitiveness in the military arena and put them at a disadvantage against adversaries who continue to develop such technologies. On the other hand, a number of international players, including NGOs and humanitarian institutions, are calling for much tighter restrictions, or even an outright ban on these weapons. They stress the risks of dehumanising conflicts and violating international humanitarian law.

In this context, the role of the United Nations becomes all the more crucial. As the world body capable of organising dialogue between States, the UN has a unique legitimacy to facilitate discussions on the regulation of SALA. The UN has a long tradition of mediation in matters affecting international peace and security, and has experience of setting up legal frameworks for the regulation of conventional weapons, such as chemical or biological weapons. However, the regulation of SALW requires a new approach, as it involves complex technological issues, modern warfare dynamics and unprecedented ethical concerns. The United Nations Conventional Weapons Forum (CCW) has been an important forum for these discussions, but persistent differences between the major powers, as well as the growing urgency of the situation, mean that substantial progress remains elusive.

For the UN, one of the major challenges lies in its ability to reconcile diverging interests and promote solutions that meet both the security concerns of states and ethical and humanitarian imperatives. This requires a subtle balance between protecting civilian populations, maintaining regional stability and encouraging technological innovation. In orchestrating these international discussions, the UN will have to work not only on establishing binding agreements, but also on confidence-building and transparency measures between States, in order to reduce the risks of uncontrolled proliferation of these technologies.

Another major challenge is to define rules and criteria to guide the use of SALA while minimising the risk of abuses. A legal framework that respects the human and ethical principles of warfare will need to include not only strict controls on the development of these systems, but also verification and accountability mechanisms to ensure that their deployment and use respect the fundamental rights of individuals, particularly in times of conflict. In addition, international cooperation instruments should be put in place to monitor and control SALA deployments, in order to prevent abuses.

Thus, although the regulation of SALAs is a complex task fraught pitfalls, it is essential to prevent abuses that could further destabilise the international system. The path to effective and balanced regulation will undoubtedly involve a gradual commitment on the part of States, ongoing dialogue and the establishment of mutual confidence-building measures. The role of the UN will be decisive in this process, acting as mediator, facilitator and guarantor of the ethical and legal principles that should underpin the use of these technologies in armed conflict.

CHAPTER 5

Future prospects

The continuing development of military artificial intelligence is opening up unprecedented prospects, while the same time raising major questions about the future of armed conflicts and the way in which they will be fought. Technological advances are making it possible to design increasingly sophisticated autonomous lethal weapon systems (ALWS) capable of acting with unprecedented speed and precision, and the issue of control and regulation is becoming central. States, aware of the strategic potential represented by these technologies, are investing massively in their development, accelerating an AI-based arms race that is profoundly transforming the balance of military power in the world. Faced with these changes, international players are faced with the need to anticipate the risks and adapt their regulatory frameworks to prevent the uncontrolled proliferation of AAS, which could have dramatic consequences for geopolitical stability and global security.

One of the major aspects of this evolution is the increasing speed at which AI can process data and take decisions on the battlefield. Unlike human beings, who need time to analyse a situation and react, autonomous systems are able to collect, evaluate and act in milliseconds, giving them a considerable strategic advantage. This speed of execution can enable more precise targeted strikes, reducing collateral losses and increasing the effectiveness of military operations. However, this decision-making autonomy poses a fundamental problem in terms of accountability and control. If an AI makes a decision that leads to human damage or a violation of international humanitarian law, who is responsible? The designers, the programmers, the militaries who deployed these systems, or the States themselves? This uncertainty makes it all the more necessary to regulate these technologies in order avoid situations where algorithmic errors or biases could lead to disastrous consequences.

Another fundamental challenge is the ability of AAS to operate in increasingly complex environments and to adapt to unforeseen situations. Advances in machine learning now make it possible to design systems capable of making decisions on the basis of non-pre-programmed data, giving them greater flexibility. However, this autonomy raises major challenges in terms of the predictability and control of AI behaviour. If an autonomous system is faced with an ethical dilemma or a situation for which it has not been specifically programmed, its reaction may be difficult to anticipate. This uncertainty can increase the risk of unintentional military incidents, particularly if SALAs are deployed in areas of tension where the slightest error could lead to an uncontrollable escalation of the conflict.

The increasing integration of SALAs into interconnected networks is also a major development that will transform the conduct of military operations. The future of warfare is likely to be marked by the rise of "systems of systems", where different AIs will collaborate in real time to carry out missions in a coordinated and autonomous manner. This approach, sometimes referred to as "swarm warfare", is based on the idea that several autonomous units can communicate and adjust their actions according to the involution of the terrain, without direct human intervention. While this capability may improve the effectiveness military missions, it also poses a major problem: who really controls these swarms of autonomous machines once they are launched on an operation? A loss of control, even temporarily, can have catastrophic consequences, which is why we need strengthen supervision mechanisms and establish strict protocols to prevent any drift.

This fragmentation of positions complicates the development of an international legal framework, especially as the speed of technological progress makes any attempt at regulation rapidly obsolete. To meet this challenge, some proposals aim to adopt a progressive approach, first establishing clear rules on the areas in which SALAs may be used and defining fundamental principles, such as the requirement for significant human control over any lethal action. Others suggest the creation of transparency and audit mechanisms to ensure traceability of decisions taken by autonomous systems, which would make it possible to clearly assign responsibility in the event of an incident.

Moreover, the future of SALA will also depend on the involvement of other players, not just governments. Technology companies play a key role in the development of these systems and must be encouraged to adopt rigorous ethical principles to ensure that their innovations are not used for purposes that violate human rights. Non-governmental organisations, researchers and civil society will also continue to play an essential role in exerting pressure to ensure that regulatory measures are put in place and respected. Inclusive governance, involving governments, international institutions, businesses and citizens, will be needed to provide an effective framework for the development of SALA and avoid potential abuses.

The continuous improvement in the learning and adaptation capabilities of Autonomous Lethal Weapon Systems (ALWS) represents a major technological evolution that is redefining the issues linked to their development and regulation. Currently, SALAs are mainly based on artificial intelligence models using supervised learning, where the algorithms are trained on the basis of pre-existing databases and well-defined military scenarios. This approach optimises the performance of the systems by providing them with clear references on how they should react to different situations. However, advances in machine learning and generative artificial intelligence are opening up new perspectives in terms of decision-making autonomy, with considerable implications for the control and predictability of these technologies.

Advances in reinforcement learning algorithms and deep neural networks now allow SALAs to learn continuously from their own experience, rather than being restricted to pre-determined patterns of behaviour. This means that these systems can adapt to increasingly complex and unpredictable environments, modifying their action strategy according to new data gathered in the field. This ability to adapt gives SALAs an undeniable operational advantage, particularly in terms of rapid decision-making and strategic flexibility. However, it also raises fundamental questions about human control, accountability and compliance with international humanitarian law.

Another major challenge lies in managing algorithmic biases and errors of judgement in AAS. Artificial intelligence systems, however sophisticated, remain dependent on the data on which they have been trained. If this data is incomplete, biased or unrepresentative of the realities on the ground, the decisions taken by AARS can be erroneous, with potentially dramatic consequences. For example, a poorly trained algorithm can confuse a civilian with a combatant or misinterpret a situation as an imminent threat, resulting unjustified loss of life. Improving the learning capabilities of SALA does not necessarily guarantee greater compliance with the rules of international humanitarian law. On the contrary, increased autonomy can exacerbate the risks if these systems are not subject to rigorous and continuous controls.

Faced with these challenges, a number of regulatory approaches are being considered to control the development of SALAs and limit the risks associated with their growing autonomy. Some experts advocate the establishment of "technological safeguards", which would involve incorporating mechanisms to limit autonomy into the very design of weapons systems. This would involve, for example, imposing systematic human validation protocols before any lethal action is taken or including automatic deactivation systems in the event of unexpected behaviour. Other proposals suggest the introduction of "non-autonomy zones", where the use of SALA would be strictly prohibited, particularly in environments where it is particularly difficult to distinguish between civilians and combatants.

The growing integration of military artificial intelligence systems into interconnected networks is one of the most decisive developments for the future of armed conflict. While today's autonomous lethal weapon systems (ALWS) are still largely conceived as units operating individually, the current trend is for them to be integrated into larger architectures, where they will interact in real time with other autonomous systems, intelligence and command infrastructures supported by PIA. This development marks a fundamental shift in the way armies design and conduct military operations, and raises new strategic, ethical and legal issues.

One of the most revolutionary aspects of this development is the concept of "swarm warfare", based on the cooperation of multiple autonomous units operating in a coordinated fashion. In the future, SALAs will no longer simply be individual drones deployed for targeted strikes or reconnaissance missions, but will operate as a network, sharing information in real time and adapting their behaviour collectively as the terrain evolves. The idea behind this approach is to mimic the way in which natural swarms operate, such as those observed in insects or schools of fish, where each individual contributes to the movement and decisions of the group without there necessarily being a single leader.

In a military context, this technology would enable fleets of autonomous drones to attack a target simultaneously, conduct large-scale surveillance operations or saturate enemy defences with diversionary manoeuvres. Such an approach offers a considerable tactical advantage: by combining advanced sensors and algorithms, these swarms would be able to analyse the environment in real time and adapt their strategy dynamically, without requiring constant human intervention. This would give them a speed execution and responsiveness far superior to those of traditional weapons systems, where every action has to be validated by a human operator.

However, this development also raises a number of concerns, particularly with regard to the responsibility for actions carried out by these interconnected systems. In traditional warfare, responsibility for military decisions is clearly attributed to an identifiable chain of command. However, with swarm warfare and the integration of SALA into autonomous networks, it is becoming increasingly difficult to determine who, or what, is responsible for a specific action. If a swarm of autonomous drones carries out an attack that results in collateral damage or a violation of the laws of war, how can the entity responsible be identified? Can the human operator who initially gave the deployment order be held responsible if the swarm makes an unexpected decision? Or does responsibility lie with the engineers who designed the drone coordination algorithms?

This difficulty in identifying who is responsible is all the more worrying given that autonomous systems are increasingly capable of modifying their own strategies in response to changes in the terrain. Unlike conventional weapons, which operate according to predetermined, fixed rules, a SALA swarm can, for example, adjust its trajectory, modify its targeting priorities or reconfigure its formation according to the information it receives in real time.

Such flexibility, while strategic, can also lead to unforeseen behaviour, increasing the risk errors and even major accidents if the algorithms malfunction.

Another challenge posed by the growing interconnection of SALAs is that of cyber security. The more interconnected military systems become, the more vulnerable they become to cyber attacks, which can be used to manipulate or hijack swarms of autonomous drones. A hostile actor, whether a state or non-state group, could potentially interfere with the communications of a SALA swarm and take control of it, turning the technology against its own developers. The risk 'military piracy' therefore becomes a major issue, requiring the development of robust countermeasures to guarantee the integrity and reliability of networked autonomous systems.

Faced with these challenges, several avenues of regulation are being considered to provide a framework for the integration SALA into interconnected networks. One proposal is to impose restrictions on the degree of autonomy that these systems can enjoy in combat situations. For example, some recommendations call for human intervention to remain mandatory for all lethal decision-making, thus preventing swarms of drones from launching attacks without prior validation by an operator. Another approach is to improve the traceability of algorithmic decisions, so that it is possible to trace the precise progress of a military action and identify those responsible in the event of an incident.

Adapting the international legal framework to technological developments in autonomous lethal weapon systems (ALWS) is a major challenge that requires a proactive and ongoing approach. Faced with the rapid progress of artificial intelligence applied to defence, States and international organisations must anticipate the emerging challenges and propose appropriate regulations avoid potential abuses and irresponsible uses of these technologies. One

of the central points of this reflection concerns the acceptable degree of autonomy of SALA and the need maintain human control over critical decisions.
One of the principles most often mentioned in this context is that of "meaningful human control". This would ensuring that no life-or-death decision is taken completely autonomously by an AI system, and that human intervention remains a fundamental requirement for any military action involving the use of lethal force. This approach aims to preserve the ethical and legal values that underpin international humanitarian law, by ensuring that human beings remain the final arbiter of critical decisions. However, the practical implementation of this principle raises a number of complex issues, particularly with regard to the exact degree of supervision required and the way in which this control can be exercised in combat situations where speed execution is crucial.
Another area for regulation is to define specific frameworks limiting the use of SALA to certain environments or military contexts. For example, restrictions could be imposed on their deployment in densely populated areas or in asymmetric conflicts where the risk of collateral damage is particularly high. Precise rules could also govern their use in strictly defensive missions, where they would be used to intercept imminent threats rather than carry out offensive attacks. Such an approach would make it possible mitigate some of the risks associated with autonomy of SALAs, while retaining the operational advantages they can offer in specific military scenarios.
Another fundamental issue concerns legal responsibility in the event of violation of the rules of war by an autonomous system. Today, international law is based on well-established principles of accountability, which make it possible to identify and punish those responsible for abuses or war crimes. However, in the case

of SALA, the question of responsibility becomes more difficult to decide: who would be held responsible if an autonomous weapon made a mistake or caused unjustified loss of life? The military operator who deployed it? The engineer who designed the decision algorithm? The company that manufactured the system? Or the government that authorised its use? The lack of clear answers to these questions makes it more difficult to establish a solid legal framework, and highlights the need to improve the traceability and transparency of the decisions made by these systems.

Finally, it is important to stress that the adaptation of the legal framework to AAS cannot be fixed once and for all. Given the speed of technological advances in the field of artificial intelligence, the rules will have to evolve constantly to adapt to the new realities of the battlefield. A flexible and dynamic approach, combining unchanging fundamental principles with regular adjustments in line with technological innovations, seems to be the best way of guaranteeing the ethical and responsible use of SALA.

One of the major concerns associated with Lessor autonomous lethal weapon systems (ALWS) is the lack of transparency and traceability of their decisions. As these technologies become more sophisticated and capable operating autonomously, the need for greater oversight becomes all the more pressing. It is essential that the decisions taken by these systems are not based on opaque processes that are impossible to explain or analyse a posteriori. This is why the development of algorithms that can be explained, i.e. artificial intelligence systems whose operation can be understood and justified by experts, is a priority area of research.

Today, one of the main challenges posed by military AI is the nature of certain so-called "black box" algorithms. These models, particularly those based on deep learning, produce results without it always being possible to identify precisely the logical path that led to a given decision. Applied to autonomous weapons, this phenomenon can give rise to considerable risks: if an attack carried out inappropriately, or if civilians are wrongly targeted, it would become extremely difficult to understand why the algorithm acted in the way it did and, above all, to determine who was responsible. To avoid this problem, the development of explainable algorithms would ensure greater transparency and make SALA decisions understandable to military operators and supervisory bodies.

One of the solutions envisaged is to impose regular audits of AI systems used for military purposes. These audits, carried out by independent bodies, would make it possible to check that the algorithms comply with precise criteria relating to compliance with international humanitarian law and the rules of military engagement. They could also include rigorous simulations and tests assess the ability of these systems to distinguish military targets from civilian populations and to react ethically in the event of an unforeseen situation. The introduction of compulsory certification, making authorisation for operational deployment conditional on validation by a regulatory body, would also provide an additional guarantee against abuse.

Another crucial aspect of transparency is the need to keep detailed records of decisions taken by SALAs in operation. The traceability of actions carried out by these systems should be an unavoidable requirement, in order to enable subsequent analysis of incidents and to ensure that sanctions can be applied in the event of a breach of the rules of war. This would involve setting up electronic logs recording all stages in the decision-making process of autonomous systems, with the possibility for judicial and military bodies to consult them in the event of a dispute. This type of system would offer a form of digital accountability, where

every action taken by a military IA could be traced and justified, thus reducing the risks of misuse or uncontrolled use.
With this in mind, some experts are calling for the creation of an international SALA register. Such a register would make it possible to centralise information on the development, deployment and use of these systems by the various States, thereby contributing to greater transparency at global level. Each country would be required to declare the types of autonomous weapons it possesses, the contexts in which they are used and the measures put in place to regulate their use. A register of this kind would make it possible to monitor the evolution of military arsenals and avoid an uncontrolled arms race, by fostering a climate of trust and dialogue between nations. It could also serve as a basis for international discussions on the regulation of SALA and the limits to be imposed on their use.
However, there are several obstacles to setting up such a register. On the one hand, many states remain reluctant to reveal sensitive information about their military capabilities, for fear of compromising their strategic advantage. Secondly, without an effective verification , a register based solely on voluntary declarations would run the risk of being incomplete or biased. To get round these difficulties, an intermediate approach could be envisaged, consisting introducing declaration obligations backed up by independent inspections, along lines of what already exists for chemical and biological weapons within the framework of^ Organisation for the Prohibition of Chemical Weapons (OPCW).
One of the other major challenges linked to SALA transparency concerns cooperation between governments and private players. Many advances in the field of autonomous weapons are now the result of collaboration between governments and technology companies, which makes the issue of regulation even more complex. The companies involved in the development of military

AI play a key role in the way these technologies are used, and their participation in defining ethical and legal standards is essential. In this context, shared responsibility can be put in place, requiring companies to respect clear commitments in terms of transparency and respect for humanitarian law.

Furthermore, the involvement of civil society and non-governmental organisations in monitoring developments in the field of SALA could provide additional leverage to ensure greater transparency. Independent institutions could be tasked with monitoring Involution autonomous arsenals and reporting any abuses, thereby helping to maintain an informed public debate on the issues surrounding these technologies. The establishment of international forums dedicated to discussing advances in autonomous weaponry and their ethical implications would also help to encourage a more democratic and inclusive approach to the regulation of AAS.

Finally, the issue of transparency and traceability cannot be dissociated from the need for greater international cooperation to provide a framework for these technologies. The United Nations, the European Union and other intergovernmental organisations can play a central role by setting up multilateral initiatives aimed at promoting common standards for the transparency of autonomous weapons. The negotiation of binding agreements on information sharing, monitoring of arsenals and traceability obligations could represent a key step towards better control of SALA on a global scale.

The transparency and traceability of autonomous lethal weapon systems are fundamental to ensuring the ethical and responsible use of these technologies. The development of explainable algorithms, the introduction of independent audits, the creation of an international register and the involvement of businesses and civil society are all avenues that can help to avoid uncontrolled proliferation and strengthen trust between nations. Without these safeguards, there is a great risk of seeing the emergence of a future in which SALAs operate without control or supervision, with potentially disastrous consequences for international security and respect for human rights.

The future of autonomous lethal weapon systems (ALWS) will not be determined solely by technological advances and international regulatory efforts. It will also depend on the geopolitical dynamics and military strategies adopted by the major powers. Competition for supremacy in military artificial intelligence has become a central element of rivalry between states, making any attempt to establish a universal legal framework particularly difficult. As SALA becomes a key element of modern defence doctrines, the most technologically advanced nations are reluctant to limit their own development in this field, for fear of losing a strategic advantage over their potential adversaries.

This competitive dynamic makes it particularly difficult to reach a global consensus on the regulation of SALA. While some countries advocate a total ban on these weapons, believing that they present unacceptable ethical and humanitarian risks, others consider that any attempt to limit their development would be detrimental to their sovereignty and defence capability. As a result, international negotiations on this subject have come up against a fragmentation of interests, with each major power seeking to preserve its freedom of action while preventing its adversaries from gaining a decisive technological lead.

In this context, it is likely that the future of AAS will be marked by the emergence of regional regulatory frameworks rather than the adoption of a binding universal treaty. The European Union, for example, has already expressed its desire to promote a more ethical approach to military AI, with restrictions designed to strictly supervise the use of autonomous systems in combat situations. Some Member States are campaigning for a complete ban, while others are arguing for strict regulations guaranteeing permanent human control over lethal decisions. This divergence of views reflects the tensions that exist on a global scale and which complicate the implementation of harmonised regulations.

In addition, the proliferation of asymmetric conflicts and hybrid wars increases the temptation for certain States and armed groups exploit SALA as a means of compensating for military disadvantages. In a world where conflicts are no longer limited to confrontations between regular armies, the growing availability of autonomous technologies is changing the strategic balance and making these weapons particularly attractive to non-state actors. Terrorist groups and militias may seek to use them to carry out targeted attacks, making the need for international cooperation in the control and monitoring of these technologies all the more pressing.

Another aggravating factor is the possibility of uncontrolled proliferation of SALA, particularly if States start exporting these weapons to third countries without a strict regulatory framework. As has been observed with armed drones, once a military technology becomes widely available, it becomes extremely difficult to control it. The proliferation of SALA can therefore fuel regional tensions and exacerbate the risks of escalation in already unstable areas such as the Middle East, South Asia and Eastern Europe.

The absence of a global regulatory framework may also lead to the emergence of "grey areas" of the law, where States or private entities develop and use SALA in contexts where the existing rules are unable to guarantee effective control. This situation could give rise to scenarios in which certain nations apply strict regulations on their own territory while authorising the development and export of these weapons to other countries with less regard for the ethical implications. This fragmentation of the regulatory framework would contribute a climate of instability and uncertainty, where the absence of common standards would make it more difficult to prevent abuses and abuses.

The future of Autonomous Lethal Weapon Systems (ALWS) cannot be envisaged without the active involvement of non-state actors, whose role will be decisive in drawing up the ethical and legal standards governing these technologies. Technology companies, particularly those specialising in artificial intelligence and military aeronautics, occupy a central place in this debate, as they are at the origin of the advances that are making these systems increasingly powerful and autonomous. It is therefore imperative that these companies are required to respect strict principles in the design and use these technologies. This means drawing up binding ethical charters, greater transparency in their development processes and a commitment not to supply these technologies to actors likely to use them in a way that contravenes the norms of international humanitarian law.

Some leading companies, such as Google and Microsoft, have already taken a stance on the military use of artificial intelligence, expressing reluctance to participate in the development of autonomous weapons without human control. In 2018, Google withdrew from renewing its contract with the Pentagon for Project Maven, a programme aimed integrating AI into military data analysis, after a strong internal mobilisation of its employees. This type of protest underlines the importance of civil society in monitoring technological advances, and highlights the role that artificial intelligence engineers and researchers can play as a counterweight to decisions that could lead to ethical abuses. However, not all technology companies share these concerns. Some, motivated by economic and strategic interests, continue to

work closely with governments and armed forces to develop advanced technologies, making it essential to establish binding international regulatory framework.
The involvement of NGOs and human rights organisations is also crucial in ensuring that humanitarian considerations remain at the heart of discussions on SALW. Organisations such as Human Rights Watch and Amnesty International have been campaigning for a total ban on these weapons for several years, arguing that they pose unacceptable risks of violating human rights and international humanitarian law. The Campaign to Stop Killer Robots, a movement of NGOs, researchers and public figures, has emerged as an influential voice in the debate, calling on states to adopt an international treaty banning AAS before their use becomes widespread. These initiatives are essential to maintain the pressure on governments and international institutions to take concrete steps towards strict regulation.
The scientific community also has a fundamental role to play in shaping the debate. Experts in artificial intelligence , ethics and international law regularly warn of the dangers of uncontrolled development of AAS and stress the need to incorporate ethical safeguards into their design. In 2015, more than 4,500 researchers, including major figures such as Elon Musk and Stephen Hawking, signed an open letter calling for a ban on autonomous weapons, stressing that their proliferation could trigger a new arms race and global instability. These kinds of stances help influence public opinion and encourage governments to adopt precautionary measures, even if they still come up against resistance from states investing massively in these technologies.
To ensure responsible use of AAS, it is imperative that companies, researchers and civil society play an active part in discussions on the regulation of these systems. Setting up independent monitoring committees to assess the impact of

technological advances and make ethical recommendations could be an effective way of preventing abuse. Similarly, ethical certification mechanisms, attesting that companies comply with strict standards in the development and export of SALA, could be introduced at international level to limit the proliferation of these weapons.

Finally, raising public awareness of SALA issues is a key element in ensuring that these technologies are not adopted without thorough democratic debate. Citizens need to be informed of the ethical and safety implications of using these weapons, so that they can put pressure on their governments and demand appropriate regulation. Education and media coverage of the subject can play a decisive role in shaping public policy, by encouraging decision-makers to take account of the concerns of civil society and independent experts .

Adapting the international legal framework to the rapid development of autonomous lethal weapon systems (ALWS) will require constant cooperation between States, international organisations and other stakeholders such as civil society and the private sector. Given the divergence of interests between the military powers and the challenges posed by a total ban on these weapons, a gradual approach may be more realistic than an immediate attempt to impose a binding legal framework on a global scale. This strategy would consist of putting in place partial and sectoral agreements that would make it possible to gradually regulate the most worrying aspects of SALA, while giving States time to adapt their policies and military doctrines.

A first step would be to establish specific restrictions on the use of SALW in certain geographical areas and conflict contexts. For example, an international consensus could be reached on banning these weapons in densely populated urban areas, where the risk uncontrolled civilian casualties is particularly high. This approach would be inspired by existing restrictions on the use of certain weapons, such as anti-personnel mines or cluster bombs, which have been banned or severely restricted because of their indiscriminate effects on civilian populations. By prohibiting the use of cluster bombs in environments where it is difficult to distinguish between combatants and non-combatants, the international community would be laying the groundwork for more comprehensive regulation.

In addition, agreements may be negotiated to ban or limit certain specific categories military AI deemed to be particularly dangerous. For example, systems capable of making targeting decisions without human supervision may be banned, while other types of AAS, used solely for defensive purposes or reconnaissance missions, may be subject to enhanced standards of transparency and accountability. A distinction should also be made between systems deployed on the battlefield and those used in law enforcement or counter-terrorism operations, prevent these technologies from being misused for repressive purposes or in violation fundamental rights.

Another possible approach would be to set up an international monitoring and transparency mechanism for the development and use of AAS. Such a mechanism would oblige states to declare publicly the categories of autonomous systems they are developing and to provide guarantees as to their compliance with the principles of international humanitarian law. This type of measure would help to establish a climate of trust between States, avoiding an arms race based on opacity and technological secrecy. An international SALA register, under the aegis of the United Nations, could be set up to monitor the development of these technologies and encourage good practice in terms of regulation and ethics.

For these initiatives to be effective, they must be based on fundamental principles guaranteeing a rigorous framework for the use of SALW. Legal responsibility is a central aspect: it is imperative that clear mechanisms be defined for assigning responsibility in the event of a violation of international law by an autonomous system. Currently, one of the main problems posed by SALA is the difficulty of determining who - the designer, the operator, the military decision-maker or the State - should be held responsible in the event of a blunder or war crime. Establishing precise rules on the traceability of decisions taken by these systems and on the chain of command would go some way towards resolving this issue, by ensuring that no lethal action can be carried out without a human being being accountable for it.

Transparency is another key principle that should guide the development of the international legal framework. States and companies developing AAS should be required to disclose the capabilities and limitations of these systems. The algorithms used for decision-making should be audited by independent experts to ensure that they comply with strict ethical and security standards. This transparency requirement would prevent the risks associated with algorithmic "black boxes", where the decisions of an autonomous system become incomprehensible and uncontrollable for humans.

Finally, the need for significant human control will have to be inserted at the heart of any future regulation. Many international organisations and groups of experts insist that, whatever the degree of autonomy of SALAs, a human must always be involved in the decision-making process when it comes to taking lethal action. This requirement could take the form of protocols requiring human validation before any shot is fired, or the implementation of hybrid systems, where the AI assists the military without ever taking the final decision to attack. This principle of human control would prevent future conflicts from becoming totally dehumanised and war from being reduced to a series of algorithms executing decisions without taking account of the moral and legal context.

Ultimately, the aim would be to achieve a robust international legal framework that provides a framework for the development and use of SALAs, while allowing States a certain degree of flexibility to adapt their defence policies. Cooperation between states, international organisations, technology companies and civil society will be decisive in ensuring that these weapons are not used irresponsibly or in a manner contrary to the fundamental principles of international law. Without such regulation, there is a great risk of seeing the emergence of a new era of conflict in which life and death would be taken by machines, without anyone being able to take real responsibility for them.

The future prospects for autonomous lethal weapon systems (ALWS) go far beyond the question of their military effectiveness and encompass strategic, ethical, legal and geopolitical issues that will shape the future of international conflicts. These autonomous weapons, fuelled by dazzling advances in artificial intelligence and robotics, will redefine not only the way in which states conceive their defence strategies, but also the very nature of military engagements and the balance of power between nations. As these technologies become more sophisticated and accessible, they could upset traditional military balances, leading to a profound transformation in global security.

From a geopolitical point of view, the proliferation of SALA is likely to accentuate international tensions by fuelling a technological arms race. The major powers, aware of the strategic importance of these systems, are investing massively in their development in order to maintain a decisive military advantage. The United States, China and Russia, in particular, are conducting advanced research into military artificial intelligence and are seeking integrate these technologies into their armed forces. This technological rivalry creates a risk of global imbalance, where countries that do not have these capabilities may be tempted to acquire these weapons by other means, y including via parallel markets or illegal technology transfers. The absence of a strict legal framework could lead to the uncontrolled proliferation of SALA, making these weapons accessible to non-state actors, including terrorist groups and armed militias.

Beyond binding measures alone, it is also essential to promote ethical and political reflection on the place of SALA in the conflicts of the future. Decisions concerning the integration of these technologies into armies must not be taken solely from the point of view of military performance, but also taking into account the profound implications they will have on the nature of warfare and on societies themselves. Should war be entrusted to machines? Is it acceptable for an algorithm to decide the fate of a human being? These questions, far from being purely theoretical, are at the heart of the debates that will shape the future of international relations and global security.

Finally, responsibility must not rest solely with governments and international institutions. The technology companies that develop these systems, artificial intelligence researchers and civil society also have a major role to play in overseeing the Involution of these weapons. The adoption of ethical charters by the major companies in the sector, the involvement of scientists in think-tanks and the mobilisation of public opinion will all help to ensure that the development of AAS does not take place at the expense of fundamental humanitarian principles.

So while the future of SALA remains uncertain, one thing is certain: their development will have a major impact on the way conflicts are conducted and perceived on a global scale. It is now up to decision-makers, researchers and citizens to anticipate these changes and put in place the necessary safeguards to ensure that technological advances remain at the service of international security and respect for fundamental human values. The absence of regulation or an overly lax approach could have disastrous consequences, transforming the wars of the future into confrontations in which artificial intelligence would have the last word, without regard for the ethical principles that have historically guided armed conflicts.

Conclusion

The integration of artificial intelligence into armed conflicts poses unprecedented challenges. It is imperative to strike a balance between technological innovation and respect for humanitarian law, to avoid any uncontrolled drift in the use of FIA for military purposes.

The integration of artificial intelligence (IA) into armed conflicts constriñes a major turning point in the history of modern warfare, presenting unprecedented challenges for societies, governments and the international community. The use of AI in autonomous weapon systems (SALA), surveillance drones, cyber-attacks or even data analysis algorithms to predict and direct militaries actions is radically changing the dynamics of war and introducing significant risks. This technological shift raises crucial questionsincluding how to reconcile these technological advances with respect for the norms and principles of international humanitarian law, in particular the protection of civilians, the distinction between combatants and non-combatants, and the proportionality of attacks.

One of the main challenges in integrating AI into warfare is to ensure that these technologies are not used in an irresponsible or unbridled manner. AI, particularly when used in autonomous systems, has the ability to make decisions independently, without immediate human intervention. If these systems are designed without appropriate safeguards, there is a risk that military strikes will be carried out indiscriminately, without human discernment, leading to dramatic consequences, including massive civilian casualties and flagrant violations of the laws of war. For example, if a machine is tasked with making lethal decisions, it will be extremely difficult to guarantee that this decision respects the principles proportionality and necessity, two fundamental criteria of humanitarian law.

This also raises the question of responsibility. In the event of a violation of humanitarian law, collateral damage or unjustified strikes, whose responsibility is it? If an autonomous IA decides to attack a target, without direct human intervention, it is complex determine whether responsibility lies with the state that deployed the weapon, the company that developed the system or the machine itself. What's more, the lack of transparency in the algorithms used by these systems makes it even more difficult to assign responsibility, creating a legal vacuum that can be exploited by malicious actors.

Another dimension of the challenge concerns the ethics of using AI in war. While PIA make certain military operations faster and more effective, it can also lead to the dehumanisation of conflict. The use of machines to make life and death decisions could erode the moral sense of war, where human lives are at stake.

are sacrificed in the name of strategic or political objectives. This raises profound ethical questions about the place of humans in war: can we really accept machines making decisions about the lives of other human beings, without any awareness of the seriousness of these choices? This disconnection from the human element can change the way war is perceived and reduce the moral responsibility of those who engage in it.

The speed of execution of IA, coupled with their ability to process huge volumes of data in real time, also represents a double-edged sword. On the one hand, this capability pent offer a strategic advantage by enabling more precise strikes that are less prone to human error. On the other hand, the accelerated execution of decisions can make the military decision-making process more difficult to control, creating a grey area in terms of responsibility. For example, if an IA makes a lethal decision in a matter of seconds, can we still guarantee that it has taken all the circumstances into account and respected the principles of necessity, proportionality and target distinction? What's more, AI algorithms are often designed to be increasingly autonomous and capable of adapting to unforeseen situations, making decision-making even more opaque. These decisions, which can be crucial to the lives of individuals, need to be supervised and understood by human authorities, but the uncertainty around the operation of IA in unforeseen contexts complicates this supervision.

It is therefore imperative that regulations are put in place to ensure that these technologies do not deviate from the fundamental principles of international law. International humanitarian law, in particular the Geneva Conventions and their additional protocols, imposes strict rules on the conduct of hostilities, seeking to human suffering, protect civilians and guarantee the dignity of those affected by the conflict. However, with the emergence of AI, existing conventions are no longer sufficient to govern the development, deployment and use of SALA. The challenge is to reach international agreements that take account of this technological reality while preserving human and ethical values. There is a great risk that AI will be used to circumvent the limitations imposed by humanitarian law, making it easier take military decisions that violate these principles, while being difficult to control remotely.

International negotiations must therefore evolve to anticipate this new reality. The international community must actively discuss the integration of AI into warfare conventions, by introducing Claris principles that define acceptable autonomy in weapons systems. Strict regulation should include requirements for human control in the decision-making process, impose transparency mechanisms for the algorithms used, and establish rigorous verification mechanisms to ensure that the use of AAS does not lead to human rights violations. Governments must also be urged to publicly declare their intentions with regard to the development

and use of AAS, with a view to collective responsibility.
Regulation is not just a military issue. It also concerns the social responsibility of the companies and researchers who develop these technologies. It is essential to raise awareness among private sector players, particularly the major technology companies, of the ethical and humanitarian implications of designing these systems. Dialogue between governments, technology companies, civil society and AI researchers is crucial to ensure that these advances remain aligned with fundamental human values and do not lead to an uncontrollable drift towards the military use of AI.
In conclusion, the integration of artificial intelligence into armed conflict is an area in which the tension between technological innovation and respect for humanitarian law will be increasingly marked. Technology pent bring considerable advances in efficiency and precision, but it must not be used to circumvent the fundamental principles of the law of war, in particular the protection of civilians and responsibility in the use of force. The regulation of military ΓIA is essential, not only to avoid abuses but also to ensure that technological progress serves to maintain peace and international security, and not to exacerbate violence and conflict.

ICRC: "The algorithms of war: the use of artificial intelligence for decision-making in armed conflicts", 22 February 2024.
IFRI: "De l'Ukraine à Gaza: l'intelligence artificielle en guerre", Politique Étrangère, 12 September 2024.
Jensen, Benjamin: "Information in War: Military Innovation, Battle Networks, and the Future of Artificial Intelligence", Georgetown University Press (3 October 2022), 320 pages.
Johnson, James: "Artificial Intelligence and the Future of Warfare: The USA, China, and Strategic Stability", Manchester University Press (14 September 2021), 240 pages.
Takach, George: "Cold War 2.0: Artificial Intelligence in the New Battle between China, Russia, and America", Pegasus Books (5 March 2024), 432 pages.
Rébé, Nathalie: "Artificial Intelligence: Crime, War, and Justice", Ethics International Press Ltd; New edition (15 November 2023), 360 pages.
Tangredi, Sam: "Al at War: How Big Data, Artificial Intelligence, and Machine Learning Are Changing Naval Warfare", Naval Institute Press (27 May 2021), 464 pages .
Galdorisi, George: "Algorithms of Armageddon: The Impact of Artificial Intelligence on Future Wars", Naval Institute Press (12 March 2024), 248 pages.
Masakowski, Yvonne: "Artificial Intelligence and Global Security: Future Trends, Threats and Considerations", Emerald Publishing Limited (15 July 2020), 216 pages.
Roucy, Laure de : "La guerre à l'ère de l'intelligence artificielle: Quand les machines prennent les armes, PUF (16 October 2024), 344 pages.
Evry, Marc: "La Guerre Invisible: Comment l'intelligence Artificielle bouleverse la géopolitique et redéfinit les conflits ", Independently published (17 January 2025), 88 pages.

Royani, Esti: "La loi sur l'utilisation des robots d'intelligence artificielle dans le domaine de la guerre militaire", Editions Notre Savoir (19 October 2023), 136 pages.
Dexar, Tony: "The Russia-Ukraine War as seen through the eyes of artificial intelligence: A view of the conflict from the impartíal perspective of AI through 100 questions", Independently published (29 August 2024), 450 pages.
Geiss, Robin: "Research Handbook on Warfare and Artificial Intelligence", Edward Elgar Publishing Ltd (26 July 2024) , 426 pages.
Celander, Lars: "How Drones Fight: How Small Drones are Revolutionizing Warfare", Casemate; 1st edition (August 15, 2024), 208 pages.
Scharre, Paul: "Four Battlegrounds: Power in the Age of Artificial Intelligenc", W. W. Norton & Company; Reprint edition (February 13, 2024), 512 pages.
Bugeja, Alex: "Robot Wars: Artificial Intelligence And The New Age Of Warfare", Independently published (November 17, 2024), 163 pages.
Shah, Raj: "Unit X: How the Pentagon and Silicon Valley Are Transforming the Future of War", Scribner (July 9, 2024), 336 pages.
Moor, Daniel: "Offensive Cyber Operations: Understanding Intangible Warfare", Oxford University Press (August 1, 2022), 328 pages.
Raska, Michael: "The Al Wave in Defence Innovation", Routledge; 1st edition (April 21, 2023), 264 pages.
Frantzman, Seth: "Drone Wars: Pioneers, Killing Machines, Artificial Intelligence, and the Battle for the Future", Bombardier Books; 1st edition (June 22, 2021), 288 pages.

Summary

Artificial intelligence (AI) is increasingly transforming armed conflicts by changing the way military operations are conducted. Autonomous Lethal Weapon Systems (ALWS), which can make decisions without direct human intervention, are at the heart of the debate. While these technologies offer the potential to increase the accuracy of strikes and military casualties, they also raise serious ethical and legal concerns, particularly regarding liability in the event of collateral damage or targeting errors. The dehumanisation of the decision-making process, particularly in matters of life and death, is also a major issue.

AI is also changing the dynamics of warfare, enabling greater automation of combat strategies and operations. For example, autonomous drones or military robots can carry missions autonomously, coordinating their actions without waiting for human instructions. This increases the speed of reaction in conflicts, but also makes it more complex to manage errors and illegal acts under international humanitarian law.

Regulating these technologies represents a considerable challenge for the international community. Although there is a growing consensus on the need to establish rules to govern the use of SALA, the divergent interests of the major military powers complicate negotiations. Some nations, for example, are opposed to an outright ban on SALAs, believing that these weapons can offer them strategic advantages in terms of defence.

The integration of ΓIA into armed conflicts requires a delicate balance between technological innovation and respect for ethical standards. Efforts to establish an effective international legal framework, while taking account of geopolitical specificities and humanitarian challenges, will be essential to avoid uncontrolled drift. International cooperation, transparency in development processes and a commitment to respect international humanitarian

law will be crucial in guiding the use of IA in future wars.
*

Artificial intelligence (AI) is increasingly transforming armed conflicts by changing the way military operations are conducted. Autonomous Lethal Weapon Systems (ALWS), which can make decisions without direct human intervention, are at the heart of the debate. While these technologies offer the potential to increase the accuracy of strikes and minimise military casualties, they also raise serious ethical and legal concerns, particularly regarding liability in the event of collateral damage or targeting errors. The integration of ПA into armed conflicts requires a delicate balance between technological innovation and respect for ethical standards. Efforts to establish an effective international legal framework, while taking account of geopolitical specificities and humanitarian challenges, will be essential to avoid uncontrolled drift.

FSC
www.fsc.org
MIX
Papier | Fördert gute Waldnutzung
FSC® C083411

Kolibri 360 GmbH
Ferdinand-Jühlke-Straße 7
99095 Erfurt, Deutschland
produktsicherheit@kolibri360.de

Druck:
CPI Druckdienstleistungen GmbH
im Auftrag der
Kolibri 360 GmbH
Ferdinand-Jühlke-Str. 7
99095 Erfurt